BOB LARSON

IN THE NAME OF SATAN

A
JANET
THOMA
BOOK

THOMAS NELSON PUBLISHERS
Nashville • Atlanta • London • Vancouver

PUBLISHER'S NOTE: The purpose of this book is to provide biblically based information for those interested in the subject of spiritual warfare. It is not intended to replace proper medical consultation or appropriate psychological therapy. Readers are encouraged to consult physicians and professional counselors prior to drawing any conclusions about the demonic diagnosis or physical, mental, or emotional ills. In addition, anyone attempting an exorcism should be trained and should be subject to pastoral authority and review.

Published in Nashville, Tennessee, by Thomas Nelson, Inc., Publishers, and distributed in Canada by Word Communications, Ltd., Richmond, British Columbia.

Unless otherwise noted, Scripture quotations are from THE NEW KING JAMES VERSION. Copyright © 1979, 1980, 1982, 1990, Thomas Nelson, Inc., Publishers.

Library of Congress Cataloging-in-Publication Data
Larson, Bob, 1944-
    In the name of Satan / Bob Larson
        p. cm.
    ISBN 0-7852-7881-8 (pbk.)
    1. Demoniac possession. 2. Exorcism. 3. Spiritual life—Christianity. 4. Satanism—United States. 5. Spiritual warfare. 6. Larson, Bob, 1944- . I. Title
BT975.L37   1996
235'.4—dc20   96-26046
                                                                CIP

Printed in the United States of America.
2 3 4 5 6 — 01 00 99 98 97 96

DEDICATION

This book is dedicated to those valiant victims of demonic possession who fought so bravely against evil. Though their particular stories will not be identified in this book, they will see portions of themselves in many of the narratives I've presented. They are ones who trusted God, and trusted the Holy Spirit leading me, so that their souls could be set free in the name of Jesus.

"In this book Bob Larson tells it like it is, just like the prophets of old. The devil and his demons are a reality and so are their intrusions in human lives. To believe otherwise is to be naive or ignorant of biblical truth. This book is a must for anyone in Christian ministry."

Jerry Mungadze, Ph.D., President
Mungadze Association, P.C.
Center for Treatment of Dissociative
Disorders

"In the future is will be important to have pastors, deliverance workers, and therapists on the same team, speaking the same language. I believe this book is a step in that direction. He came to set the captives free, and we are to continue His work, so thanks for the training manual."

Dr. Jim Friesen, Psychologist
Author of *More Than Survivors: Conversations with Multiple Personality Clients*

"Bob Larson's knowledge of the Bible and his many experiences in counseling have equipped him to present a realistic procedure in dealing with demonized persons. His accounts of Christ's deliverance of the oppressed are vivid and encouraging. His grasp of our authority in Christ and his compassion for those hurting enable him to share many helpful insights for those who would help to set the captives free."

C. Fred Dickason, Professor
Moody Bible Institute

CONTENTS

PART 3
Delivering Those with Demons

ACKNOWLEDGMENTS

Special thanks to my wife, Laura, who edited the manuscript and offered helpful suggestions. Her special flair made the narratives come to life. Thanks to my dedicated staff who worked so hard to provide me time to write this book. Special gratitude is due to those pastors and friends, my spiritual mentors, who have encouraged me onward in spiritual warfare: Dr. Jerry Prevo, Dr. Terry Smith, Rev. Ross Johnston, Bobb Biehl, Dr. Tim LaHaye. I also appreciate those who read the manuscript and offered their beneficial comments: Dr. Jerry Mungadze, Dr. James Friesen, Dr. C. Fred Dickason. As always, thanks to Janet Thoma for pushing me onward to excellence.

INTRODUCTION

I don't normally take the time to read a book's introduction, because I like to get straight to the business of the book. I'm glad you've chosen differently. Your understanding of what follows will depend on what I say here, because this was a risky book to write.

It was risky because some might use this information with the wrong motives or wrong assumptions. I've done my best to avoid that happening. This book is also precarious for those who want to blame their emotional problems on the demonic. They may forego appropriate counseling and embark on a fruitless round of exorcisms at the hands of well-meaning but misguided exorcists. This book is also hazardous for those who think every spiritual difficulty can be corrected by delving into deliverance. Pursuing such a misdiagnosis could result in irreparable mental harm to those who seek freedom from imagined evil forces.

This book is also risky for me. I have placed myself in jeopardy of having my motives and theology misunderstood. It would be safer to stay silent, but I've spoken for the sake of those who agonize alone because few dare speak about this unique area of ministry. Victims of unspeakable demonic torment must know that others like them have suffered, and that men and women of God will place their lives and reputations in peril for them.

Empathetically embracing victims of demonic possession involves more than heeding St. Augustine's plea to hate the sin and love the sinner. It requires understanding the human fault of underestimating the devil's cunning, and thus being fooled by his strategies. Don't despise those who have fallen prey to possession by devilish powers. You may think they are morally weaker or less spiritually cautious than you, and you may be right in some cases. But remember, their story might be yours, "but for the grace of God."

The narratives I have chosen were selected because they illustrate examples of the various ways demons operate. They were not picked because they represent any particular point I wish to make or any certain doctrinal position I want to proclaim. They were the best anecdotes I could recall to emphasize what I considered important to this study.

Please note that references to demons are made in the masculine. This is appropriate with respect to biblical terminology, although a certain androgyny is inherent to the character and function of evil spirits.

Don't think that by meticulously noting the circumstances of each account of deliverance, you can decipher any specific person's case history. In the interest of confidentiality, and out of respect for those who so courageously presented themselves for ministry, I have altered certain details surrounding each person's story. In all cases names have been changed. When it did not affect the authenticity of the description, I sometimes changed the sexual identity of the person. On occasion I also modified the geographical location and other factors, while always seeking to maintain essential scriptural and factual accuracy. The basic information of each case is faithful to the original occurrence. Above all I have made certain that the spiritual dynamics of each exorcism remained exact.

In some ways I regret referring to those possessed by demons as victims. I fear it could connote a certain helplessness, which might evoke a disdainful opinion from some readers, or it may suppose a lack of personal responsibility for their state. I finally settled on using the term *victim* because I frankly could not find another suitable word. I apologize to any "victims" of demonization who may be offended by this expression. These people are gallant warriors in the struggle against evil, and their lives have been battlefields.

I say in advance to those who will microscopically inspect every Scripture I quote and each story I tell: This book is not the final word on demons and deliverance. It is the record of my journey from the safe confines of traditional ministry into uncharted realms of offering hope to the hopeless. I've made mistakes along the way, but I have done what I could, when I could, to set at liberty those who have been bruised by Satan (Luke 4:18).

If you find what's written on these pages difficult to accept, please don't judge me. Pray for me. I'm still struggling to discern God's purpose in calling me to such an awesome task. I aspire not to be an expert on demons and deliverance, but a student of the Holy Spirit, always seeking to learn more about His love for fallen humanity.

I don't have all the answers, but I do know that the spiritual battle lines of our age are not between believers of different persuasions. Christians are combatants in a conflict between good and evil, light and darkness, God and the devil. This war, against all the evil being done in the name of Satan, has already been won in the name of Jesus.

PART ONE

All the Evil

CHAPTER 1

Ceremonies in Singapore

I first encountered a demon in 1967 in the city of Singapore during a trip that changed my life in many ways. I was a young Christian man, yearning to experience the exotic sights I had only seen on the pages of travel magazines. First I went to Europe, then the Middle East, and finally Asia. For a month I trekked across the India subcontinent, from Bombay to New Delhi and Calcutta. I ended up in Southeast Asia.

Of particular interest to me were the stories of supernatural occurrences in these areas, particularly a Hindu ceremony called Thaipusam. This ritual of self-mutilation occurs every year in only two places on earth, a rural section of Malaysia, near Kuala Lumpur, and the island city-nation of Singapore.

Even in Hindu-dominated India, this rigorous ceremony of piercing and lacerating one's body is outlawed. But in 1967, Singapore was not the modern financial metropolis of international trade that it is today. In the late '60s it was still a sleepy tropical melting pot of diverse cultures and religious beliefs. This multicultural environment adopted an indifferent attitude toward the Hindu minority who practiced Thaipusam. The leaders of Singapore believed this live-and-let-live stance helped maintain religious and ethnic harmony.

I was curious to see if the descriptions I had read about Thaipusam, the act of *bloodless* self-mutilation, were exaggerated, so I set out to find a way into this secret world. After going through the normal tourist channels and finding no one who would talk about Thaipusam—much less tell me in which temple it would take place—I met a missionary who had witnessed this ceremony several years before. With his directions in hand, and the help of a curious taxi driver, I finally found the temple.

The Tank Road Hindu temple complex covered half a city block. Six-foot-high whitewashed plaster walls surrounded the temple grounds, which were accessible by a single, narrow entry. I expected some kind of security check, but was surprised to find that no one seemed concerned about who came or went.

I arrived at nine o'clock in the morning and the temple grounds were already a bustle of activity. A hundred or so penitents were in various stages of self-torture. One man had large hooks through the muscles in his back, from which he was pulling a heavy stone idol around the grounds. Another man looked like a human pincushion, with more than fifty safety pins inserted all over his face. Still another had wooden soles strapped to his feet with dozens of sharp nails hammered through and pointing upward. I grimaced as I watched him walk in circles around the compound.

In the center of the Tank Road temple was a small, ten-foot by ten-foot shrine. Half a dozen bare-chested priests, covered from the waist down with the flowing Indian skirts known as *dhotis,* scurried in and out of the shrine with flower and fruit offerings. I made my way toward them to see the object of their devotion: a three-foot-high stone pillar in the shape of an elongated cone.

I caught the attention of one of the priests and pointed toward the object. "What's that?"

"A *lingam,*" he replied in a British colonial accent. The priest noted the confused look on my face. "It's a male phallus," he explained, "a representation of the male organ. It signifies fertility and life."

Ordinarily I would have been put off by this display of religious adoration of a sex object, but my travels across India in prior weeks had educated me to the eroticism underlying Hinduism. I recalled the depraved stone carvings I had seen over the entry of a temple in northern India. Bestiality and unspeakable depictions of sexual perversion had been precisely sculpted into the stone archway so that Hindus entering the temple couldn't avoid seeing them.

When I asked the attending priest why such immoral renderings were found at a religious site, he answered, "These images help worshipers get out all of their dirty thoughts before they enter the temple."

That questionable logic introduced me to one of the conundrums of Hinduism. In some Hindu disciplines, perverted sexual practices are combined with religious devotion, as in disciplines like tantric yoga. This school of yoga teaches that religious and erotic ecstasy are reached when the mind, breath, and semen are stilled in a single moment of sexual and spiritual enlightenment. The pornographic temple sculptures I had seen weeks before helped me make sense of the offensive sight before me in Singapore.

"Are you enjoying our religious festival?"

I turned around to see who was speaking and saw a slight Indian man standing right behind me. I wasn't sure how to respond. "It's interesting," was all I could say. "What happens after these people are finished torturing themselves?"

The man motioned for me to follow him a few steps to the temple entrance. He stepped outside the temple compound and pointed down the street. "They will walk three miles in that direction and then have all the instruments of torture removed." A broad smile filled his face as he spoke with a sense of pride. "You will not see one drop of blood shed. This shows the great power of our gods."

This man, like everyone I met at the ceremony, was unusually cordial. Like a Christian witnessing for his faith, these people wanted to accommodate me so that I would be beguiled by their gods. There was no way I could question them about the logic of their ritual. They were sincere in their dedication and were proud to display their devotion.

As I stepped back inside the compound a band of musicians began moving about the crowd. One man blew on a flute, which made a mournful, almost atonal sound. He was accompanied by several men with drums, hanging from slings around their necks. Each man had his fingers covered with hard, round cylinders that beat rhythmically against the heads of the drums. The almost mystical sound evoked images of a snake charmer, and I half expected a mesmerized cobra to rise somewhere off the temple grounds.

What bothered me most about this religious spectacle was that children were allowed to be present and watch the events. A dozen or so of them imitated their elders. Although their self-mutilation wasn't as severe, it appeared to be no less excruciating. Their backs and chests were pierced with dozens of pins and their arms bore signs of painful slashes. Several of them sat passively in a circle, seemingly indifferent to actions that under other circumstances, in other cultures, would have constituted the most severe forms of child abuse.

I wandered about the Hindu temple grounds until I came upon a devotee named Raja. Raja, who had journeyed to Singapore from Madras, India, told me that the previous year he had prayed to the Hindu gods to heal his ailing father. When his father's illness had subsided, Raja vowed he would travel to Singapore and fulfill his pledge. To prove his piety, he had stripped to his waist and sliced his exposed body parts with sharpened knives. His tongue was pierced with a six-inch-long ice pick.

More than a hundred, three-foot-long, pin-sharp skewers also pierced his body. The skewers were supported by a device called a *kavadis,* which consisted of metal braces strapped to his shoulders. Though the skin was lacerated, true to the testimony of the penitents, not a drop of blood appeared. All this self-torture was done to honor the Hindu goddess Kali.

How could a person's skin be punctured in dozens of places without bloodletting? How could a person endure such pain and still function? Why was there no infection surrounding the wounds? My mind was filled with questions and horror, but I was left speechless by such human degradation in the name of devotion.

I walked to one side of the temple grounds where a six-foot-tall stone idol of Kali stood before bowing worshipers. Kali's entire body was painted black. One of her feet was perched on a dead body, while she held the severed head of her victim in her left hand. Around her neck hung a necklace of human skulls, her other victims. Her eyes were enlarged and distended, like many other pagan idols I'd seen on my travels.

Passing Hindus expressed their adoration for Kali by draping her arms and neck with garlands of flowers. I shook my head in disbelief and ached in my heart for Raja, who had credited such a frightful goddess with supernatural curative powers.

As I made my way back toward Raja, I noticed that he was accompanied by a young Indian who held a copy of sacred Hindu scriptures and chanted from the text as an encouragement to his friend. This young man read with an enthusiasm that bordered on mania. Suddenly his face contorted, his eyes bulged out, his head jerked back, and he let out a deafening scream. He crumpled over in writhing convulsions, as if some force had thrown him to the ground. His eyes rolled back in his head as his limbs jerked and flung about in the dirt. Other Hindu supplicants rushed to his side. They shouted at each other frantically in their native Hindi language.

"What happened?" I asked a Hindu who was standing nearby.

"The spirit of the goddess entered him," the man answered. "We know, because Kali always affects us like this when she comes."

The young Hindu seemed to be in torment, and I couldn't help but notice his eyes! They looked like the eyes of the stone goddess. Now I understood why many of the heathen idols had such protruding eyes. It was a sign of the evil spirit's presence.

That look haunted me for months to come, and it became an important clue when attempting to detect spirit possession. In subsequent travels I saw it in the eyes of Haitian witch doctors during voodoo ceremonies when they called forth the *loa*. I saw it in the eyes of Brazilian macumba adherents as they aped the actions of animals. I spotted it near Kathmandu, Nepal, as *sadhus*, Hindu holy men, sacrificed goats to the Hindu god Shiva. And I witnessed it in Fiji as fire walkers stood unharmed in the midst of flaming coals.

All of these ceremonies, though called by different names, and though separated by thousands of miles, served the same master: Satan.

That day in Singapore profoundly shaped my view of the spirit world. The fact that I saw hundreds of devotees pierce their bodies in the most grotesque ways *without a drop of blood being shed* showed me the power Satan has over those who willingly submit to his kingdom. And the way in which I reacted when faced with a soul-rending demon made me realize God's anointing—a unique deportment in the presence of evil.

I returned to the United States and devoted myself to an intensive study of demonic phenomena for the sake of communicating what I saw to the body of Christ. I devoured every theologically sound book on the subject and searched the Scriptures for biblical incidents that would shed some light on how to deal with demons. My prayers were an open invitation for the Lord to use me in confronting evil spirits, but it took three years before I finally encountered a demon on American soil. That happened in the city of St. Louis, Missouri.

CHAPTER 2

The Evil Spirits of St. Louis

One night in 1971, three years after my trip to Singapore, I spoke at a Youth for Christ rally in a suburban St. Louis church. At the conclusion of the evening, a group of teenagers surrounded me to debate certain points in my message. As the conversation was about to conclude, a fifteen-year-old girl named Ann approached me.

She was short, with cropped blonde hair. Her arms were folded. "I don't believe in your God," she challenged me. "I'm an atheist." Her voice sounded cool, confident, and determined.

Without thinking I responded, "Do you believe in the devil?"

"Yes!" she insisted.

"Why?"

"Because I *feel* him."

By now the other youth surrounding us had backed off, irritated by her intrusion. I motioned for them to leave us alone and pointed for Ann to step to the side of the church platform.

"What did you mean by saying you *feel* the devil?"

A leering smile crossed her lips. "I have sex with the devil," she answered.

I was unprepared for her answer. Back then, I had never heard of incubus, demonic sexual intercourse in which a spirit assumes male proportions and sexually stimulates a human female. Frankly, I thought she was trying to impress me by her impudence. Just in case there was any truth to her story, I decided to find out more. I asked her to follow me into a nearby Sunday school room, and sent someone to tell Bill, the Youth for Christ rally director, to join me.

Minutes later the three of us sat facing each other with our chairs in a triangular position. I began with a series of questions about Ann's spiritual condition. In contrast to her belligerence a little earlier, she seemed to alternate between intense antagonism and nonchalance, often staring into space as if I was not there. She would reply to my questions about her spiritual beliefs in words that carefully avoided the name of Christ.

If I had been more experienced in such encounters, I would have known several ways to expedite the proceedings. I would have kept my eyes on her and insisted as politely as possible that she not take her eyes off me. I would have used conversation with biblical phrases that could incite a demon, such as "the blood of Christ" and "the victory of the Resurrection," along with testimonial references to what Christ meant to me.

After nearly an hour of fruitless dialogue, I decided that Ann's story was serious enough to warrant a final attempt to contact a demon. Like most people wondering if they might be on the verge of an exorcism, I was hesitant. Who wants to attempt such an incredible accusation and be wrong? However, it was worth any embarrassment to set Ann free.

"Ann, in the name of Jesus," I started, not really sure of the exact words to use, "I demand to talk to the devil within you."

The Youth for Christ director leaned toward me and whispered in my ear, "I've been through this sort of thing before, and I'll help in any way I can."

I looked at him, relieved. I was grateful to know I could get some coaching, but wished he had said something earlier.

At first my entry into the domain of exorcism seemed a failure. Ann showed little reaction to my demand. Maybe I hadn't spoken forcefully enough.

"Didn't you hear me?" I asked the unseen presence. Borrowing language from a couple of books I'd read about exorcisms, I insisted. "I told you to come forward and talk to me, whoever you are."

This time Ann's head jerked backward and her body stiffened, just like the young Hindu boy in Singapore. Her eyes closed, her face contorted, and her fingers flexed as if something inside her was trying to come out.

When Ann's eyes opened, they widened with that same fiendish look. "What do you want with me?" a deep, masculine-sounding voice replied. "Leave me alone. Her body belongs to me!"

What struck me immediately was that the voice was not her own. It had a clipped, British accent. Three years earlier, on that trip around the world, I had stood in London's Hyde Park and listened to the Sunday afternoon, soapbox speakers as they spouted obscenities, poetry, and blasphemies. As a result, I could detect a genuine English accent.

"Ask his name," Bill directed me.

I sat forward in my chair, drawing myself to my full height as if that might be more intimidating. "In Jesus' name, tell me who you are."

"Miss Love," the spirit replied with a smirk.

I looked at Bill. He shook his head.

"Well, whoever you are, are you British?"

"Oh yes. I've even inhabited royalty."

Whether or not the comment was truthful, it was still remarkable for a fifteen-year-old girl from a rural Missouri community to speak in a male voice that sounded like an actor in a BBC sitcom.

"Do you really love her?" I asked.

The hands of Miss Love seductively caressed Ann's legs and thighs. "Of course. She's married to me. She's mine, all mine."

"Bring Ann back," Bill whispered.

Acting as if I knew exactly what to do, I ordered, "Spirit, I bind you in the name of Christ and command you to go down. Let Ann come back."

Miss Love shot an annoying glance at Bill and then reluctantly acquiesced. After what appeared to be an internal struggle of some sort, Ann's body gradually relaxed, her face softened, and her personality returned. It was amazing to see the spirit's obedient response to the spoken authority of Christ's name.

"Ann, I believe what you told me about feeling the devil inside you. You're possessed by a demon, and I'm going to cast it out!" As I spoke those words, I realized I had never done this before. Cast out a demon named Miss Love? I wasn't even sure who Miss Love was, let alone know how to proceed further. But my mentor, Bill, was sitting calmly beside me. And I knew there was a connection between that day in Singapore and this night in St. Louis. Thaipusam was God's way of introducing me to the reality of the supernatural.

I expected Ann to resist what I had suggested. Instead she dropped her head and spoke softly, "It's no use. I'm married to Miss Love and he owns my body."

Why didn't the spirit call himself Mr. Love? I knew that in the Bible, angels and demons were always referred to in the masculine gender. *Perhaps Miss Love is the demon's way of referring to Ann, not himself?* I thought.

Ann jumped to her feet and began pacing about the room, wringing her hands and gesturing erratically. "Help me, help me!" she cried one moment, followed by, "I want Miss Love, I like what he does to me!" the next.

"Sit down," I finally demanded, and Ann plopped herself into the steel folding chair.

I decided more had to be known before we could get Ann's cooperation. Then I experienced something that in later years of conducting exorcisms I would covet prayerfully. God spoke through me without any deliberate forethought on my part. "Miss Love, you're going to kill Ann, aren't you?"

This time the demon abruptly manifested. "How did you know that?"

I didn't have an answer. The thought was not my own.

"How are you going to kill her?"

Miss Love raised one eyebrow and cocked his head haughtily. "She'll hang from a tree, just like your Jesus!"

"Does Ann know this?"

"Of course. I've convinced her she has to die like Christ. She already has the rope and knows where the tree is."

"When?"

"Soon, very soon," Miss Love bragged.

"You can't have her, and you won't kill her!"

Miss Love crossed one leg over the other and shifted sideways in the chair. "Well, well, well, look who's talking," he taunted me. "You don't even know what you're doing— without help from your friend over there," he said, gesturing toward Bill. "Anyway, I know all about you."

As a young Christian I was still sensitive about my failures before coming to Christ. This was my chance to stand on the promises of God's Word and let my faith speak for itself.

"You're right, I haven't always lived for God. But that's in the past, forgiven. Jesus did something for me at the cross you'll never experience."

"I don't want to hear about that!" Miss Love screamed, maintaining that same precise British accent.

"Fine, then get out of here!"

"I won't go. I don't have to go as long as she doesn't know about . . ."

"About what?"

The demon in his bravado had obviously said something he shouldn't.

"In Jesus' name, tell me what she needs to know."

"That stuff."

"What stuff?"

"All that salvation stuff you're talking about."

Looking back on that night from the perspective of hundreds of exorcisms later, I still marvel at how God intervened to make the demon say what I needed to know. Discovering what the victim of possession needs to say or pray to be free is a key to victory in exorcisms, and the information is usually obtained only after a laborious interrogation. It's like assembling a puzzle, involving life-and-death pieces. In this case, God mercifully allowed a divine shortcut to set Ann free.

The demon, knowing he had spoken out of turn, glared at me and faded away. When Ann returned, she was even more docile. What had taken place internally had weakened Miss Love's dominance.

"Please help," Ann pleaded. "I don't want to die."

"Then you do know about the . . ."

"The hanging? Yes, how do you know?"

"Never mind. It's just important for you to know that you don't have to die. Christ has already died for you."

I took a Bible and started through the Scriptures, explaining how Ann could know Christ personally. As later exorcisms taught me, such a situation normally evokes disruption. God's Word will usually cause the victim severe internal pain or the person will try to flee. This time, God dramatically intervened, and the only interference I could see was the overwhelming feeling of sleepiness that overcame her.

I assumed this reaction was because of the late night hour, which neared midnight. I learned later that induced slumber or mental fogging is a common distraction used by demons. Ann fought the sleepiness and assimilated what I was saying. She acknowledged each scriptural step of salvation. She prayed, asking Christ to enter her.

The prayer didn't come easily. At one point, I had to lead her word by word to overcome Miss Love's hindrance. When the last words of Ann's salvation prayer were spoken, the demon abruptly returned.

Now the evil spirit was less defiant than before, knowing his hold on Ann's life had been broken. "Think you're pretty clever, don't you?" the demon said. "But you still don't know who I really am, do you? Miss Love is what I call myself. That's not the name given to me by my master. Why, you even talked about me tonight."

Tonight? That was an odd thing to say. I thought about what I had said in my message that night in St. Louis. The focus was about the rock opera *Jesus Christ Superstar*. To me, the musical was blasphemous, pure and simple. Its depiction of Judas as a hero and Jesus as an ambivalent messiah who was involved with Mary Magdalene and doubted His calling was evidence of satanic inspiration. Christian young people needed to reject the seduction of popular culture's portrayal of their Savior.

"What do you mean, I talked about you? Who are you? If you're not Miss Love, what's your real name?"

"You can read all about me in the thirteenth chapter of Revelation."

I reached for my Bible and read aloud: "I saw a beast rising up out of the sea, having seven heads and ten horns, and on his horns ten crowns, and on his heads a blasphemous—"

"Blasphemy!" the spirit broke in. He threw back his head and laughed sarcastically.

Blasphemy! That's why he said I spoke about him tonight. Jesus Christ Superstar *is blasphemous!*

As if he read my mind, the spirit said, "Would you like me to quote a few of my favorite lyrics from that sterling opera

I helped inspire? You do recall that the men who wrote *Superstar* were British?"

Before I could react, Blasphemy began quoting line after line from at least a half dozen *Superstar* songs. I knew that this was not an act by a fifteen-year-old girl who had memorized song lyrics, learned to effect an upper-crust British inflection, and perpetrated a hoax on me. The demon who stared from Ann's eyes exuded hatred for God and all that was good.

The spirit continued. "Miss Love . . . even *she* thought that's who she was. She thought I loved her, so I nicknamed her Miss Love, and took the name for myself too." Blasphemy looked at me insolently. "Pretty ingenious, wouldn't you say, old chap?"

The demon's flippant attitude seemed odd at the time. Through the years I've learned that some demons like to brag about their trickery. Sometimes I allow them to boast. Often they become overly confident and reveal something I wouldn't have known otherwise.

"Check to see if Blasphemy is the only demon," Bill said to me softly.

I demanded that Blasphemy tell me what other evil spirits were inside Ann. Reluctantly he divulged that there were six others. Ann's demons of lust, murder, and incubus each had names personifying their purpose. A demon named Monica puzzled me. Why did it have a human name? When we called Ann from the demon's trance, we learned that Monica was a girlfriend who had introduced Ann to the occult through the Ouija board and satanic rituals.

Bill taught me to start with the weakest demon and work upward, thereby depriving the top demon from drawing strength from those under him. (This may not be the most efficient way, but it works well in some cases.)

He also showed me how to cross-examine each spirit to find out its name, how it entered Ann, and then finally to lead Ann in a prayer, renouncing the sin of entrance. We then forced each spirit to pronounce his own doom by saying his name and declaring, "I renounce my claim to Ann, I obey the judgment of God, and I go to the pit." The entire procedure took hours.

Throughout the process, Blasphemy continually intruded, knowing we were closing in on him. When all those under him were gone, we faced Blasphemy.

As a novice, I asked the demon if he was indeed the actual demon described in chapter 13 of the book of Revelation.

Blasphemy found my ignorance amusing. "Thanks for the compliment," he responded. "No, that one is yet to come, but my deeds have earned me the right to bear that name."

In subsequent exorcisms I have encountered demons named Satan, Lucifer, Beelzebub, and a host of other names taken from Scripture. What I learned that night in Missouri revealed to me that certain names in Satan's kingdom refer to a rank the spirit holds. Satan has apparently arranged a hierarchy like that of the military, with sergeants, lieutenants, generals, and so on. At the top of these levels are often the powerful demons: Lucifer and Satan. They are fallen spirits that have excelled because of their successful debaucheries. (Apart from Judas and the Antichrist, there is no biblical evidence that Satan ever possesses a person.)

Weakened by the lack of assistance from those under his authority, Blasphemy left much easier than I had anticipated. When he was gone, Ann jerked suddenly and came to her senses, with a look on her face we had not seen all night, an angelic serenity. Gone too was the sultry demeanor and the contentious attitude. She had only the sketchiest idea of what had happened and wasn't even sure where she was.

What struck me most was the ease with which she spoke the name of Jesus. When I had led her in a confessional prayer at the start of the exorcism, four hours earlier, she was only able to utter the name of Jesus, syllable by syllable. Now she said "Jesus" with a joy that came from her deep spiritual yearnings.

THE "SHOW ME" STATE SHOWED ME

That night in St. Louis taught me valuable lessons. Most important, God didn't allow me to encounter the evil spirits alone. Without Bill at my side I certainly wouldn't have proceeded with confidence. And the exorcism might have lasted much longer than it did, so long that Ann might not have obtained full freedom.

Since then, I have been involved with hundreds of exorcisms. Some have lasted no more than a few minutes, while others have gone on for hours, weeks, months, and even years. Some demons have been almost benign to the point of wanting to leave rather than risk being battered by a servant of God. Others have fought vigorously and violently. Still others are bewildered by why they possessed their victims. Most fought skillfully and determinedly.

As you read this book and wonder if you might ever be thrust into a circumstance similar to the ones I will describe, I can assure you that God will not allow you to entertain such evil unaware of what to do. Furthermore, the purpose of this book is not to train you in deliverance, but to help you with your everyday Christian life. By understanding how Satan operates in the arena of the supernatural, you will be better prepared to thwart his advances.

I invite you to follow me into a realm few Christians dare to enter. You'll explore the meaning of evil and discover the best ways to resist cults and the occult. You'll learn how to wage spiritual warfare by confronting Satan's kingdom. As a practical matter, you'll find out how to bind evil spirits, loose angels, and cast out demons. You'll read many stories about actual exorcisms I've encountered, so we can demystify the procedure of deliverance.

Be careful you don't presumptuously engage in spiritual warfare. If you do, the protection of God's guidance might be excluded, as it was with the seven sons of Sceva (Acts 19:14–16). These arrogant exorcists tried to cast out demons without the apostle Paul's knowledge and authority. They didn't know Christ and acted in self-confidence. Demons attacked them and physically overpowered and disgraced them.

My prayer is that you'll understand that spiritual warfare isn't the exotic stuff of missionary stories, and it isn't the distorted caricature of Hollywood horror films. It's the command of Jesus and a privilege every Christian can experience. When you realize what Jesus meant by trampling on serpents and scorpions (Luke 10:19), you'll uncover a new life of faith in our God—who is big enough to handle anything the devil can do!

CHAPTER 3

The Devil Made
Them Do It

Henry Lee Lucas's life of crime began when he stabbed and strangled his seventy-four-year-old mother before raping her dead body. By the mid-'80s, Lucas was considered one of the most notorious serial killers of our time. He claimed to have killed 360 people using, as he said, "most every way but poison." He admitted to shooting, stabbing, burning, beating, strangling, hanging, and crucifying his victims. Yet Henry was convicted of only three murders, including that of his common-law wife, Becky Powell, whom he killed when she was only fourteen.

As of 1996 Lucas spends his days on death row in a Texas penitentiary. Technically, he is sentenced to die for the death of one person, and he now claims the 360 number was inflated to titillate authorities. The truth will probably never be known, but Henry knows why he did what he did. He says the devil made him do it. At least that's what he told me face-to-face.

Before Lucas was remanded to the Texas state penal system, he was housed for a short while in a small jailhouse in central Texas. Lucas heard my nationally syndicated radio broadcast and asked to meet with me.

Sitting in the cell with a condemned killer, without anyone in sight, was one of the eeriest experiences of my life. Lucas had nothing to lose by harming me, so I was understandably uneasy. I listened for hours as this uneducated drifter spun yarns about child abduction and white slavery cults.

Though Lucas said he never went beyond grade school, he seemed quite bright. He described in detail the way he dispatched various victims, and how underground satanic death cults trained him. I didn't know then—and I still don't know—how much of that is to be believed. But the one thing I do believe is that Satan controlled Henry Lee Lucas's life. He said so unequivocally, and his life of crime bears testimony to some out-of-control malevolent force within him.

Henry told me how he would murder one victim after another for days on end. He was indiscriminate in his targets. Some were children he'd abducted from playgrounds. One woman was raped and killed in a shopping center parking lot. Hitchhikers were the easiest to kill, and Lucas had forgotten how many of them had died at his hands. Lucas killed men, women, and children of all races and classes.

Henry put it this way. "At the time of the murders I was completely numb. I was like an ice cube. It was like being out of my body, almost like being unconscious. It felt good. I couldn't even see the person's body lying there. All I could see was an image.

"As long as I was near the body, I couldn't get my feelings back. So, to keep on killing without remorse, I would cut off part of the body and carry it with me while I went on to commit other crimes. One time I drove for days with a man's head, covered by a coat, lying on the passenger seat of my car."

I wanted to call for a guard, I was so repulsed by what he was saying, but I stayed because Henry said I was the one person he wanted to know the whole story.

"I would kill as many as ten people in one day," he continued with an icy stare. Henry looked at me to see my reaction to his revelation. He had an eerie gaze, since one eye was fake. I had trouble believing that he could muster the energy and the evil cunning to kill ten victims in one day! When he murdered, Henry must have been truly a crazy, demon-possessed man.

I glanced around the room to see if there were any sharp objects at his disposal.

Lucas must have known what I was thinking. "Don't worry," he said. "They won't even let me have a mirror in here." He pointed to a polished piece of flat metal hanging on the bars. "That's what I use to see myself when I shave . . . and I have to return the razor they give me when I'm finished."

I motioned for him to go on with his story.

"I went days without sleeping," he continued. "Then, when I got rid of the body part, I could finally quit killing and go to sleep."

"Why did you do it, Henry? Was it for the thrill of killing or was there some larger purpose?"

"I didn't mean to kill my mother. She tried to hit me, and I struck back. It was the same thing with Becky. I was overcome with rage and . . ." His voice trailed off in a tone that sounded like regret.

"What about all the others you killed?"

"They were different." Henry leaned forward, and his voice lowered to nearly a whisper, as if he were afraid someone might hear him. "All the others I killed were done for the satanic cult I became part of."

I sat back in my chair, somewhat skeptical. Serial killers like Henry Lee Lucas are notorious con artists and telling the truth isn't something they do with consistency. Typically, they deny the evil they do and the pain they cause their victims.

"You have to kill to get into the cult," Henry explained. "As a satanic ritual, a child was kidnapped once a year and crucified alive. Our purpose was to reincarnate the devil as the ruler of earth. In exchange, the devil allowed me to go undetected. I even passed lie detector tests. I would sit across the street and watch the police investigate my victims, but no one ever questioned me. I wouldn't be in this cell today if I hadn't turned myself in."

Henry wasn't the first person to tell me about the murderous activities of secret satanic cults. His details of ritual killings squared with everything others had related. He described how victims were systematically tortured to prove the loyalty cult members had to Satan. The particulars about certain sexually depraved ceremonies were so similar to narratives I'd heard from ritual abuse victims it was uncanny.

Psychiatrists and even playwrights have come up with their own explanations for Lucas's crimes: suppressed homosexuality, the abusive upbringing of his prostitute mother, and his penchant for attention, which could only be satisfied by being exceedingly bad. Yet during the long hours we conversed, Henry returned again and again to the theme that Satan had made a pact with him, and he fulfilled his part of the agreement by murdering his fellow human beings.

Others insist that Lucas is just a storyteller, cleverly attributing the responsibility for his murderous actions to an unidentifiable cult. That may or may not be true, but I believe some want to ignore what Henry says because they can't admit that more than genetic and social influences skew certain people toward the dark side. No one could kill his mother and wife in cold blood and not have a serious evil influence.

As I spent those long hours in Lucas's cell, one thought came to me again and again. *Henry Lee Lucas was at one time a harmless child.* What made him into a merciless killer? Are there other Lucases growing up in homes where the evil around them is indoctrinating them into a life of aberrant behavior? What makes them become so disturbed in their minds, emotions, and spirits?

There are answers for some of these questions. Other potential serial killers are just waiting to happen. They are consumed with a combustible mixture of anger and rage, and who knows what spark will ignite their crime spree. The absence of love in some families is so heartrending that one instant of rejection, one blow to the body, one rebuff at a time of emotional vulnerability, one employer termination is all that's needed to create another Henry Lee Lucas. No one will ever know what goes on inside the homes and hearts of these people, the full extent of the evil that is harbored there.

I found three recent stories in the news especially troubling.

UNSETTLING EVENTS IN THE NEWS

In Silsbee, Texas, eleven children, ages eight to fourteen, harassed and chased a horse in a pasture for hours until he dropped from sheer exhaustion, tangled in barbed wire. Mr.

Wilson Boy was an old brown horse that no one would normally think of harming. No one, that is, except these eleven youngsters. When the owners of Mr. Wilson Boy arrived on the scene, they found their beloved quarter horse lying on the ground with a broken leg and sharp sticks rammed up his nostrils as the children's final bit of torture.

The youngsters, who clubbed the horse to death, returned to their elementary and junior high classes the next day and laughed about what they had done. They even thought it was "cool" to be arrested at school. Their remorselessness shocked the 6,300 residents of Silsbee, where the most common offense was a traffic ticket.

This cruel and senseless slaughter of a beautiful quarter horse raises the disturbing question: How were these children raised that they would do such a thing? Residents claimed they were all from "normal" homes.

The same question might be asked of thirty youths at a Castle Rock, Colorado, keg party. Tanked on beer, a group of teenagers stumbled upon what they thought was an unconscious, injured man. Unbeknownst to them, the person they abused was already dead. One of the group even urinated on the corpse, and then they left it without notifying anyone. Not one of the youngsters called to get help.

The local sheriff commented, "I've been in this business twenty-eight years and this is shocking. It really makes you wonder about kids today." In the aftermath, the only thing that could be done was to charge one of the participants with the abuse of a corpse. Again, these were the children of upstanding families.

Another more serious case involved two teenagers in White Cloud, Michigan, who killed a seventy-three-year-old man, then partied and showed his body to at least ten friends. The police didn't learn of the incident until four days later when relatives discovered the remains. The citizens of White Cloud were left to wonder how so many kids could witness a murder victim's body and not tell the authorities or even their parents.

I am bothered, of course, by the serious crimes involved in these incidents, especially the murder of the man. I am also concerned about the apathy exhibited by the young people who saw the evidence and did nothing. Such flagrant disregard says something dangerous about the rationale these young people live by. Can you imagine what reaction you would expect if someone showed a corpse to your child?

Most who hear about such horrible deeds point a finger at the home. They say there is a breakdown of the family. That's true, but we need to be more specific. The heart of the problem is the dismissal of God from the daily lives of parents and children. That is the true evil among us.

Confronted by the problems of the family, politicians blame a broad array of national ills and promise more money, at taxpayers' expense, to right such wrongs. Psychologists fill the news reports with sound bites about abuse statistics and grim deductions forecasting social disintegration. Reporters and columnists suggest any number of solutions.

Some point to the influence of the media and Hollywood, which have certainly stoked the fire by making heroes of villains. Consider, for example, movies like *Natural Born Killers* and *Pulp Fiction*. But if Hollywood cleans up its act, will that alone heal the home? I don't think so. Unfortunately, the problem is rooted deep in our society.

WHAT IS EVIL—DO WE KNOW ANY LONGER?

Horrific occurrences like those in Silsbee, Castle Rock, and White Cloud get buried in the back pages of our newspapers because the idea of evil is not easily accepted by today's culture. The mention of it does creep into our language occasionally. For example, President Bill Clinton called the Oklahoma City federal building bombers "evil cowards." In another instance, President Ronald Reagan was at first vilified, and then lionized, for helping to bring about the downfall of what he called the "evil empire"—the Soviet Union. Shakespeare scripted Mark Anthony's speech over Julius Caesar's body with the words, "The evil that men do lives after them." His audience of Londoners probably understood the notion of evil better than most psychiatrists—and most of us—do today.

Let's face it, evil as a moral concept isn't all that popular. When actor Hugh Grant was caught soliciting oral sex from a prostitute, the best explanation he could offer Jay Leno on *The Tonight Show* was that there are good things and bad things, and he did a bad thing! He acted like his fornication was just a silly game. What didn't seem to concern him was how his actions may have influenced other youth struggling with sexual sin. Worse yet, society just laughed it off.

Even the dictionary is no help in clarifying the word *evil*, for it uses synonyms like *sinful* and *wicked*, words that are equally taboo in our age.

It's not enough to talk about evil in ambiguous terms, like Supreme Court Justice Stewart Potter, who defined pornography by saying, "I know it when I see it." A humanistic culture may never put its finger on what makes men do evil things. Still, that doesn't stop most from concluding that men do evil, and something—or someone—encourages them to do so.

The real tragedy is that few of the custodians of our culture are willing to say conclusively what is right and wrong. None will suggest there is anything like ultimate truth. They avoid using absolute moral terms like evil and sin because they are believed to be too judgmental for our "enlightened" culture.

When considering the behavior of the youth in Silsbee, Castle Rock, and White Cloud, I am bold enough to suggest that the devil made them do it, and their parents allowed the devil to do so!

This doesn't exonerate the youth from responsibility for their actions. "Each of us shall give account of himself to God," Romans 14:12 reminds us. To credit Satan as the origin of evil isn't the same as conceding to comedian Flip Wilson's amoral ethic, "The devil made me do it." Instead it gives the devil his due by admitting that human depravity alone can't account for the sheer outrageousness of some sinister deeds.

The higher-self advocates of our modern world have convinced many that cruel insensitivities are more the failure of people not yielding to the better angels of their nature than our being tempted by an evil adversary. I often wonder what these "seek your inner divine consciousness" types would say to a victim of satanic ritual abuse who has told me of being buried alive in a coffin filled with snakes, surviving only by the use of a breathing tube sticking out of the ground. Would a New Ager argue that the cult members who perpetrated this atrocity were merely out of touch with their true spiritual nature?

What about the five-year-old who told me that satanists held her hands tightly around the handle of a dagger, which was plunged into the heart of her playmate? Her innocence was destroyed by the demon-possessed members of a generational Luciferian cult whose leaders believed such depravity was the only way to please their lord, the devil. These satanists were driven by the indwelling presence of evil, not merely the absence of good.

To the non-Christian, cruelties like the Cambodian killing fields is beyond rational accountability. The thought of three million people being genocidally slaughtered and their corpses hurriedly thrown in mass graves is unfathomable. The nonbeliever can only conclude that someone like Pol Pot, the communist Khmer Rouge leader who perpetrated this evil, was insane or genetically aberrant. The humanists who dominate our age cannot bear to think that someone who directed the torture and murder of millions was inhabited by dark forces.

As for me, it's obvious I believe Satan is real. Whether or not our society chooses to acknowledge him doesn't change the fact that evil is ultimately embodied in a personal, malignant creature who tempts, torments, oppresses, and possesses humans.

WHO IS SATAN?

The identity of the devil is shrouded in myth, often eclipsing the biblical reality of a personal creature devoid of goodness. In literature and legend he is known as the Adversary, the Prince of Darkness, Slewfoot, Mephistopheles, and Old Scratch. The Bible refers to him as Satan, Lucifer, and the devil, the progenitor of pride, instigator of avarice, font of folly, source of seduction, origin of temptation, and evocator of evil. Human language seems inadequate to characterize what is unthinkable to the human conscience: absolute immorality incarnated in depravity.

Ezekiel 28:13–17 describes in detail his original state. He was exquisitely clothed, a master musician, and an anointed angel of the cherubim class who walked in the presence of God. He knew the perfection of Eden before the Fall and caused the stars to dance with his symphonies of adoration before God's throne. He was so beautiful that his very radiance became the source of pride that led to his fall.

From Isaiah 14:12–15, we learn that sometime after Creation, the idea lodged in Satan's heart to be like God, the Most High. As a result, war raged in the heavens, and Satan was successful in persuading at least one-third of heaven's angels to concur with his insurrection (Rev. 12:4). Since that time the devil has roamed the earth seeking vengeance upon the Almighty by tempting and ravaging man, the beloved of God's creation. Lucifer's emissaries of evil, the corrupted angels who rebelled and fell with him, are demons doing his bidding to oppose God's eternal purposes.

THE VALUE OF ACCURATE INFORMATION

My goal is to provide you with inside information on how the devil's kingdom of darkness operates so that you can effectively combat him when the need arises. In the world we live in today, you can be sure that someday, somewhere, that time will come.

In the heat of the spiritual warfare of an exorcism a demon once taunted me, "You'll never be able to speak about what went on tonight. No one would believe you, and that's our most powerful tool." If I have learned anything in all my years of dealing with demons it is that satanic spirits count on the human incapability of imagining anything so evil as they are.

What starts out as just a little evil, like the killing of Mr. Wilson Boy, the quarter horse, can eventually grow to gigantic proportion. We cannot let "the devil made them do it" be the final spiritual epitaph of this generation. If we as a society can comprehend the cause for some of the outrageous behavior pervading our culture, we can begin to cure it.

CHAPTER 4

The Evil That Demons Do

Fifteen-year-old Andrew Merritt calmly loaded a shotgun in his upstairs bedroom, then tiptoed downstairs where his mother lay sleeping on the couch. He placed the barrel of the gun to her head and shot her twice. Then he and a friend left her body where it was and fled in her car to Mexico.

Only a few miles into the trip, one of the car tires blew out and stranded the boys in the middle of a field. Andrew used his mother's car phone to notify authorities about what had happened. Police found him looking at the photo on his mother's driver's license, with tears streaming down his cheeks. "The devil made me do it," was all that he muttered as they handcuffed him and took him to jail.

Andrew told his lawyer that Satan had appeared to him out of a fireball, which came from a black hole, as he listened to the death metal band Megadeth singing a tune entitled,

"Go to Hell." ("My only friend's the goat, with 666 between his horns.") The devil told Andrew to hasten his demonic return to earth by killing all Christians, and to begin with his mother, who was a devout Christian.

His lawyer, a man who personally explained the case to me, put it this way: "Whether or not Andrew saw the devil, or thinks he did, really makes little difference. The music made him think he was in contact with something evil that took control. He believed it enough to kill for it. I'm faced with the fact that the influence of Satan can't be considered a mitigating influence in a court of law, and we have no effective defense for the case."

Today, Andrew languishes in a mental institution. His suicidal impulses are controlled by daily drug injections, and his hallucinations about the devil are stronger than ever. If he ever sees the outside world again, it won't be until after his forty-fifth birthday. He will certainly need extensive spiritual counseling to heal his troubled soul if he is to survive on the outside.

Andrew was a seemingly normal boy from a good Christian home. He may have had deeper psychological problems with one or more members of his family; but on the surface, we assume this tragedy should not have happened, not in this family. However, I believe other forces were at work in the Merritt household, undermining all the good intentions of Andrew's Christian upbringing.

I've met many young people who have been swayed by Satan. They are primed by adolescent rebellion and fueled by the anti-parental invectives of heavy metal rock lyrics; sometimes they fantasize about eradicating their parents so they can gain control over their lives. Most youth pass through this dangerous phase and move on to a more sane outlook. A dangerous few allow these obsessions to dominate their thinking.

In the hundreds of cases of demon possession I have dealt with, I can cite several dozen that involved teenagers who seriously considered killing their parents. When I faced their demons directly, the evil spirits told me of the detailed murder plans. Was there a man or woman of God who missed the chance to intervene in Andrew Merritt's case?

I met Andrew's pastor, the minister whose church Andrew's mother also attended and the man who conducted her funeral. I believe he was sincere when he told me, "I never saw anything that could have warned me of such consequences. If Andrew's mother could speak from the grave, I'm certain she would warn Christian parents not to assume that what happened to her couldn't happen to them."

I believe that crimes like those of Andrew Merritt could be curtailed if we understood how evil influences our lives. It's so simple if we'll just face it directly! Evil comes from the influence of the world, the flesh, and the devil and his demons.

THE WORLD

In spite of his diligence to oppose God's kingdom, Satan isn't sufficient in himself. The adversary is limited in time and space and he isn't omnipotent, so he must use a number of fallen spirits to do his bidding. He's playing for big stakes and may not send a particular demon on a mission to seduce one human. Therefore, he relies on the evil influence of his extended world system to pervert human behavior.

Christians often refer to the influences of "the world" as

"worldliness" and quote as their pretext: "Do not love the world or the things in the world" (1 John 2:15). Friendship with the world is enmity with God, James 4:4 tells us.

When asked what the "world" is, most Christians respond with specifics, referring to whatever behavior their particular religious tradition has labeled as worldly. But specific behavior, such as drinking, smoking, dancing, and substance abuse, does not represent the world's system of spiritual conflict.

The true battle with evil is described clearly in the Bible. Ephesians, chapter 6, tells us that "principalities," "powers," and the "rulers of the darkness of this age" are in charge of our world. This Scripture refers to Satan's system of supernatural activity, which is organized spiritually and geographically. Certain principalities control particular countries and cities. (For example, Daniel 10 refers to the spirits "prince of Persia" and "prince of Greece.") Other powers direct their attention to designated sectors of society, such as the political and academic realms. Rulers of darkness focus on certain industries like entertainment and pornography. Demons with specialized abilities work their evil where they are most effective.

Our world has fallen from Eden, and all humanity is overshadowed by the cosmological consequences of sin. That domination is most evident in popular culture. When Bruce Willis and Arnold Schwarzenegger glorify violence in their films, they aren't just actors for hire. They are bit players in a sinister drama.

It's no wonder Andrew Merritt and other teenagers credit rock songs and singers as a major source of their values. Way back when Mick Jagger pleaded for "Sympathy for the Devil" at the 1969 Altamount Rock Fest, pop culture turned a corner on the highway to hell. Today's death metal bands aren't just the clever marketing tools of the black end of the rock musical spectrum; the lyrics and lifestyles of these bands are the cutting edge for the Antichrist's coming war on the saints.

THE FLESH

The devil often sits back and lets the flesh do his dirty deeds. Unrestrained human sexuality can turn the beauty of intimacy into something ugly through pornography. In this case, the fallen nature of man's evil desire turns humanity toward evil without any active intervention from Satan. As James 1:14 points out, "Each one is tempted when he is drawn away by his *own* desires" (emphasis added).

Blaming everything on the devil is a precarious cop-out. The flesh—man's own lust—can accomplish much evil without active demonic intervention. On death row, serial killer Ted Bundy confessed that the influence of pornography had driven him to murder. When the homes of child molesters are raided, the police seldom find stacks of the *Wall Street Journal*. What they discover is hard-core porn, the obvious link to their perverted behavior.

The temptation of Christ in Matthew 4:1–11 clearly shows that the devil also directly appeals to our human weaknesses. Jesus had fasted forty days and forty nights when Satan tempted Him by suggesting that He turn stones into bread. This was a straightforward appeal to His hungering body. Today, men and women with human weaknesses are tempted by the images of erotic sexuality that flood our newsstands and saunter across the screens of our television sets. "Sex sells," isn't an advertising slogan born on Wall Street; it's an epigram conceived in the depths of hell based on temptations of the flesh.

In order to ward off the seductive appeal of the flesh, we need to lean on the promises of God to overcome our internal propensity to sin. The murder of Andrew Merritt's mother might have been prevented if young Andrew had truly understood the significance of 1 Corinthians 10:13: "No temptation has overtaken you except such as is common to man; but God is faithful, who will not allow you to be tempted beyond what you are able, but with the temptation will also make the way of escape, that you may be able to bear it." But then again, he may have committed his mind to Satan beyond the normal ability to resist temptation.

As I've just pointed out, some will sin as a result of the world's wretched standards of ethics and morals. Others will yield to temptation because their own flesh draws them inexorably toward depravity. But some may not fall into Satan's plans, even though the world and the flesh tempt them. These are the ones who need an extra inducement from the devil and his demons.

THE DEVIL AND HIS DEMONS

I believe that much of the degeneracy of our age is the direct result of the devil and his demons, who are dedicated to the goal of arousing desire for the forbidden. So what are these demons like?

What Is a Demon?

The very mention of the word *demon* conjures images of gargoylish creatures of the night—complete with fangs, claws, and backs hunched by the weight of depravity. Many victims of possession claim they can see such creatures. Whereas our "normal" eyes cannot behold the spirit world, those who give themselves to the occult can somehow see beyond this veil or else have demon-induced visions.

On some occasions when demons have appeared during an exorcism, the victim has described the spirit as incredibly beautiful. This reminds us of Paul's warning in 2 Corinthians 11:14: When it suits his purposes, the devil can transform himself into an "angel of light."

But this visible manifestation of a demon says nothing about the actual nature of these fallen angels. Both secular and religious history are filled with references to demons. The ancients, who were untouched by the Jewish scriptures, held demons in superstitious esteem. Animists placated them as capricious forces to be appeased, lest they retaliate in mischievous ways. The Greeks believed demons were the spirits of departed wicked men.

Three theories: Pre-Adamic race, mongrels, or fallen angels
Some Bible scholars say that demons are either the spirits of a pre-Adamic race or the offspring of evil angels who cohabited with human women (the Genesis 6 theory).

The pre-Adamic theory states that in Genesis 1:1 God created a perfect earth at some indistinguishable point in the past. According to the theory, between verses 1 and 2 of the first chapter of Genesis, a cataclysm occurred, which was God's judgment on evil humanity. The spirits of this wicked race were disembodied and roamed the earth seeking humans to possess.

The cohabitation hypothesis is based on a unique interpretation of Genesis 6:1–2: Evil fallen angels sexually commingled with certain human females before the Flood. This perverted union resulted in mongrels who were part human and part demonic, the genetically mutated giants of Genesis 6:4. The flood subsequently destroyed the natural bodies of these monsters, leaving their spirits to seek human possession and habitation.

I agree that Genesis 6 describes a sexual linkage between demons and humans, which produced humanoid offspring. That is one reason for the severity of God's judgment in destroying the earth with a worldwide flood. However, I also believe that the death of these creatures at that time ended both their physical existence and their spiritual freedom. They were sent to a special prison (2 Peter 2:4; Jude 6).

In all my years of dealing with demons, I have never encountered a case that contradicts my conclusion about the origin of evil spirits: They are angels who fell from their estate as did Lucifer (Ezek. 28:11–19; Isa. 14:12–15). Approximately one-third of all created angels succumbed to the devil's plea of insurrection against God (Rev. 12:4), and they are now his emissaries of evil (Matt. 25:41—"the devil and his angels").

Free vs. confined to hell   There is some evidence that the angels who fell with Lucifer are relegated to one of two states. Some appear to be free to roam the earth in search of human prey, while others are confined to Tartarus, or hell (2 Peter 2:4). The sin that confined these demons isn't clear from Scripture. Perhaps Jude, verse 6, refers to these demons ("angels who did not keep their proper domain . . . He has reserved in everlasting chains"). This may indicate that they are the ones who sexually cohabited with humans in Genesis 6.

The question "What is a demon?" must also address the nature of their character.

The Unique Degeneracy of Demons

Demons were created in God's image as was man, who is "a little lower than the angels" (Ps. 8:5). Consequently, demons have intellectual prowess and a will that determine their conduct. This individual distinctiveness extends to their personal identity. Each demon has a name and the capacity to speak (except in the case of mute demons). They also possess considerable emotion. James 2:19 describes them as not only believing in God, an indication of intelligent conviction, but also trembling at the thought of divine existence.

Wherever demons are spoken of in Scripture, they are depraved ("unclean"—Matt. 10:1; "wicked"—Eph. 6:12; "evil"- –Luke 7:21). Even though I've heard the voices of thousands of demons as they responded to my demands in the name of Christ, not one has ever expressed any desire to be different from what he is. Demons have listened while I led their victims to Christ, but no demon has ever asked to be a recipient of God's grace. Their condition is obviously one of unique degeneracy, a predicament that consigns them to a permanently unclean condition. In short, no demon can ever be saved from sin. Demons have no equivalent payment for sin on their behalf. Furthermore, not one has ever expressed any regret for his actions.

The moral nature of demons compels them to ceaselessly oppose God's kingdom and fight against His redeemed servants. They do so as invisible creatures, even though they may manifest visibly on occasion, just as the angels of the Lord appeared to man (Gen. 19:15; Luke 1:26). Though they may assume a mask of righteousness and beauty, the Bible illustrates that their true image is ghastly and abhorrent (Rev. 9:7–10).

The Supernatural Power of Demons

As you will discover in this book, demons have extraordinary supernatural powers. Their physical strength far surpasses that of mortals. The demoniac of Gadara was so strong that shackles and chains couldn't confine him. He broke them in pieces and "neither could anyone tame him" (Mark 5:4).

This supernatural power extends itself to acts that seem to defy all natural laws of physics. Second Thessalonians, chapter 2, warns of the "power, signs, and lying wonders" that demons will manifest during the Tribulation. These paranormal phenomena include the healing of a wound that inflicts death (Rev. 13:12), creating fire that falls from heaven (Rev. 13:13), and animating a material object so that it speaks as if it were human (Rev. 13:15).

Demons are not bound by physical barriers. A legion of demons dwelt inside one man (Luke 8:30), indicating that thousands of them can coexist simultaneously in the same confinement. Perhaps they are no more than minute dots in space, lending some credibility to the ancient conjecture that many angels can dance on the head of pin.

Demons are obviously not bound by spatial limitation since they can enter the material body of a victim. They can also travel from one location to the next almost instantaneously. I have dealt with demons who summoned assistance from spirits in other countries and these unclean spirits appeared almost instantaneously.

The most important thing to note about the nature of demons is their consistent devotion to Satan's purposes and their unilateral opposition to God. Because of this, they express complete certitude about spiritual matters. No demon I've dealt with has ever denied that the Bible is God's inerrant Word. None have ever questioned the deity of Christ or His authority over them. Their character is consistent: utter contempt for their victims, bitter hatred for the person ministering deliverance, and absolute loathing for Jesus and the Holy Spirit.

Demons incite sin in the hearts of the morally weak: lust, homosexuality, pedophilia, and adultery. That's not to say that every such vice is necessarily demonic, but it may be more times than we are willing to admit.

I have an important question for every parent reading this book: When was the last time you talked to *your* children about the devil? Could it be that Satan and sex are the two most taboo subjects in the Christian home? I'm not suggesting that Christian families be preoccupied with negative discussions about what the devil does; however, most Christian parents will have to admit they seldom, if ever, take time to tell their children there is a real devil who seeks to seduce, especially those who follow the Lord.

Our children must have a sense of sin and a comprehension that Satan is seeking to steal, kill, and destroy. They need to be told how despicable Satan is, and how clever he is in his plans to deceive them. The purpose for such a conversation is not to have our children focus on evil things. Our emphasis should be to keep the eyes of our families on things that are "true . . . noble . . . just . . . pure . . . lovely . . . and praiseworthy" (Phil. 4:8). But the Bible also commands us to "expose" the "works of darkness" (Eph. 5:11) and be "wise as serpents" (Matt. 10:16).

Children need to know that evil spirits sometimes cause perverted behavior. It's not enough to warn them to avoid immoral actions.

Can Someone Have a Demon Without Knowing?

"Can a person have a demon and not know it?" may be one of the most fundamental questions asked about deliverance. The answer is yes. In fact, when people calmly ask me if they have a demon, their inquiry is usually an indication that they do not. While demons may feel obligated to challenge me while I am praying with a person, they will not normally advertise their presence if they are not threatened.

Some who are possessed *do* know that they have demons because they have seen them. These people usually have come out of a background in the occult where specific demons were summoned and appeared upon invocation. Others may know they have demons because they hear voices in their heads. Certain individuals can actually hear conversations between various demons. Other persons lose time because of demons having put them in a trance, and they wonder if such oblivion is the result of an evil spirit's presence. (Hearing voices and losing time can also be a symptom of dissociative disorder, which will be discussed in Chapter Nine.)

Generally, the person who has a demon knows he has serious spiritual problems that have defied all of his efforts to rectify. He may even have wondered if the root of his difficulties might be demonic. Most have never given serious consideration to the thought they are possessed. After all, who would really want to contemplate such a conclusion?

CHARACTER OVERCOMES THE DEVIL

One of the things that has amazed me about demons is that some people have committed inconceivably immoral acts without being controlled by demonic forces. I have known individuals who have gone so far as to offer human sacrifices in the name of Satan—yet demons, it seems, were never able to enter them. Other victims of the devil became possessed with seemingly lesser sins. Eric was one of them.

I encountered Eric while I was speaking in a strict fundamentalist Baptist church. He approached me, saying that an unusual anger had overcome him as I spoke. He wondered why he hated me so intensely, when as a devout Christian he should have been pleased by my presentation.

Later as I spoke to him I caught a flash of the demonic look in Eric's eyes, and found it a strange contrast to his reticent demeanor. Eric was slightly built and seemed to lack self-confidence. The demon's gaze was belligerent and spiteful. The change was so complete, no actor could have mimicked such a radical personality transformation. With Eric in a trance, the evil spirit defiantly confronted me with a loathing I have seldom seen, even in the case of outright satanists.

The most curious thing that I discovered about Eric's possession was how it occurred. Months earlier, on his high school prom night, he lost his virginity in the backseat of a car. "That's when I entered him," the demon of lust explained.

I realize that many other teenagers have fallen into sexual sin and in some cases lived inordinately promiscuous lives, without ever granting a demon the right of entry. Why was Eric so easily overcome by such a common sin? I'm convinced the answer was his lack of moral fortitude and submission, perhaps, to the spirit inhabiting his sex partner.

If the core of a person's identity is strong-willed, it seems harder for a demon to take over, no matter what that person does. On the other hand, some people are "easy." Easy to talk into anything. Easy to bend the rules, easy to hang out with the wrong crowd, easy to compromise a principle, even though they may not actually step far over the line of transgression.

Why hadn't Eric's demon spent its time inhabiting a child molester or a porn star? Because Eric was easy to invade, and the others who committed more heinous sins may not have been so compliant. That thing we call character, the defining force of our soul's will, is the final gateway to the human spirit. When the soul and character of a person has not been strengthened by a positive self-image, the constitution of that person is more vulnerable to not only the world and the flesh, but also the devil.

Parents can't supervise their children twenty-four hours a day, but they *can* instill in them a sense of godly character, a gift their children can carry inside their hearts all their lives. In a world that extols getting ahead at any cost, we must emphasize the value of ethics and absolute standards. From babyhood on, children need to be positively reinforced with a sense of their value as creations of God who are destined for spiritual greatness. They need to know they are loved and accepted for who they are in God's eyes. And they need to be prayed over, and with, on a daily basis. They will then be less susceptible to the influence of demons.

This affirmation needs to come from their parents. I believe that fathers and stay-at-home mothers play a crucial role in protecting our children. I know it is not always possible for parents to be with their children as much as they would wish, but when there is a choice between working to acquire things and spending time with one's children, the answer is easy. Spending time with your children is the best investment you can make to ward off supernatural evil influences.

I don't want to stir up unwarranted alarm by suggesting that Satan can influence any emotionally disturbed Christian kid to commit murder, as Andrew Merritt did. My goal is to speak to those who may think their rebellious offspring is just going through a phase, when the child may be in urgent need of spiritual counseling.

To protect ourselves and our children from the devil, we need to have a more perceptive understanding of what evil is all about. Evil is a matter of conduct, not just a state of mind. We must see the signs that Merritt's mother missed, and not be blind to a loved one's aberrant behavior.

I can only guess what these signs may have been. I do know from talking with Andrew Merritt's lawyer that the youngster was heavily under the influence of death metal music. In fact, his soul was so permeated, he felt Satan spoke to him through the music. The day that the song "Go to Hell" drove him to murder was not the first time he had heard it. Andrew's friend, who helped kill his mother, introduced him to bands like Megadeth.

The child who listens to lyrics of bands like Slayer, which advocate Satan worship, musicians like Glen Benton of Deicide, who admits being a satanist, and groups like Morbid Angel, which encourage fans to blaspheme the Holy Spirit, can't help but become belligerent and resentful of parental authority. Every parent should feel worthy to engage in the battle over what type of music will be allowed in the home.

My guess is that a closer examination of Andrew's life and surroundings would have produced additional clues. Most rebellious youth cover their bedroom walls with posters of satanic rock bands. They often keep a journal of occult sayings, rituals, and deeds. Their rooms may contain paraphernalia such as daggers, bones, skulls, chalices, and black candles. They may experiment with drugs and dress in black. They're especially fond of T-shirts with gruesome artwork about death and torment. This is not to suggest that any one or more of these indicators mean a teenager is about to commit a heinous act. But these warning signs should prompt parents to take immediate inventory of the emotional and spiritual health of their child.

Teenagers could be overcome by evil impulses, even to the point of contemplating parricide, without realizing how truly satanic such thoughts really are. The devil hears when they snarl under their breath, "I wish you were dead!" They may entertain thoughts of getting even in violent ways without considering that those thoughts are demonic.

We must never forget that evil is a real threat to us, and that the devil is constantly seeking to devour God's children (1 Peter 5:8)—in the name of Satan.

PART TWO

Spiritual Warfare

CHAPTER 5

Harmless Deeds, Harmful Demons

Demons show up in unlikely places, for the strangest of reasons. The demons I have encountered were not usually found in large cities where sin seems to abound; they often revealed themselves in out-of-the-way places, where you'd least expect to confront such hideous evil.

One such location was a rural Canadian community known best for its wheat crops and earth-solid prairie values. One warm spring afternoon, the churches of that area banded together and invited me to address a special youth rally. What I thought would be an ordinary day turned out to be a remarkable encounter with evil.

Almost the whole town, nearly a thousand people, turned out. They sat on wooden folding chairs arranged in front of a small stage at one end of the high school basketball gymnasium. The hometown team apparently didn't draw large crowds, so the gym had been constructed with little room on the sidelines for seats. Both sides of the court came within a few feet of abutting cement-block walls.

The crowd responded to my message in a typically Canadian manner: polite and quieter than U.S. audiences and with respectful attentiveness. I spoke about young people's need to fully surrender their lives to Christ. I barely mentioned the subject of spiritual warfare, giving only a brief warning.

"Avoid the occult," I warned them. "Even a slight brush with the things of Satan can bring lasting spiritual damage to your life. Remember, the devil plays for keeps, and he's always seeking the chance to lure you into a compromising situation. I've known teenagers who became demon possessed by doing far less than they thought would lead them to satanic bondage."

At the end of my message, I asked people to bow their heads for a closing prayer. As we did, someone screamed from the center of the congregation. I looked up to see chairs flying in every direction. The clatter as they hit the floor was like a string of firecrackers going off. Some people panicked and ran for the doors.

I focused on the cause of the disturbance. A teenager was shouting obscenities and racing around throwing chairs. He lunged at one of the cement walls and tried to scale it, clawing at the masonry with his fingernails.

A dozen or so burly farmers converged around the young man and pinned him to the gym floor. Speaking over the public address system, I asked the crowd to remain calm and told the men who had subdued the teenager to bring him forward. Then I motioned for a pastor to come near, and whispered for him to take over and dismiss the audience once I was out of the building. Meanwhile, the young man who had caused the disruption was dragged backstage, kicking and screaming.

"Is there a church nearby?" I asked. A pastor who had given the afternoon's invocation told me that the young man attended his church, and volunteered his facility. Three other pastors agreed to meet us there. One pastor commented, "The scene in the gym will probably cause the biggest uproar this town has seen since the railroad bypassed our grain silos for larger markets to the south."

We put the youngster in the backseat of a car and drove him to a white-frame building several blocks from the gym. Once inside the church, the teenager continued to thrash about, spouting obscenities. Two of the more muscular pastors pinned the teenager to the church floor just in front of the first row of pews.

"Does anyone have any idea why this young man went berserk?" I asked.

"Randy is a popular kid in town," said the pastor of the church. "He's usually cruising up and down Main Street picking up girls. He's quite the lady's man."

"He's captain of the football team," another minister added. "I just don't understand what this is all about. Randy is a quiet kid. He hardly ever says anything. Why would he act like a maniac?"

Everyone agreed that the outburst back at the gymnasium was something they would never have expected of Randy. That was sufficient evidence for me, and I took action.

I walked over to Randy, whose eyes were wild and dark. His expression looked vacant. I wasted no time confronting the devil. "In the name of Jesus, I demand to know what evil spirit made Randy act as he did."

The ministers looked surprised. My unabashed bluntness stunned them. Everyone suspected Randy's actions might be demonic, but confronting the demon head-on wasn't something they would have done. They just wanted Randy to come back to his senses.

(The reaction of those clergy is typical. I often hear preachers of the gospel refer to some heinous crime or outrageous action as "demonic." Even the secular press will sometimes refer to a particularly gruesome murder as "diabolical." But such adjectives are usually linguistic trips of the tongue, with no real intent of actually diagnosing what happened as coming from a supernatural source.)

"Now wait a minute, Mr. Larson," one of the ministers interjected. "You can't just come waltzing into our town and tell us that the most popular kid in our high school is demon possessed. Why—"

"Hang on, Hank," Randy's pastor interrupted. "You and I both know Randy is not the kind of kid who would go berserk in public and cuss like he did. Maybe Larson senses something we don't."

I did, and it was because of that look in Randy's eyes, the same one I had seen so long ago in Singapore. I immediately challenged the spirit staring at me. "I demand again to know your name. In the name of Jesus, tell me who you are!"

The men holding Randy tightened their grip. The muscles of his athletic body flexed and Randy sat up on the floor. He rose to his knees like an animal about to pounce on its prey.

Slowly and deliberately a voice came from deep within his throat. "My name is Disobedience."

"How did you enter him?"

"Through the game."

"What game?"

"I don't have to tell you!"

"You have no choice. The Lord demands that you tell me, as do all these men of God."

The spirit Disobedience glanced around the room at the ministers. He locked his eyes on each of them, trying to find one he could intimidate. In spite of their earlier skepticism, they stared back at the demon with confidence. If any one of the preachers had backed off, I don't know what might have happened.

"We rebuke you in the name of Jesus," said the pastor who had at first questioned what I was doing.

"Amen," said another.

Every pastor confirmed his agreement, which left the demon little choice. "I entered through the 'light as a feather' game," Disobedience said in disgust. "His parents told him he couldn't go out that night, but he did. He disobeyed them, and that gave me my right. Now he belongs to me."

"Spirit, I bind you in the name of Jesus. Go down. I want to talk with Randy."

The eyes of Disobedience rolled back and Randy gradually came to his senses. "What am I doing here in my church? How did I get here?" He shook his head in amazement.

After a few minutes of explaining what had happened, I confronted Randy. "Tell me about the 'light as a feather' game. When did you play it?"

"I don't know what you're referring to," he answered. "I think it's a child's game."

"What's this all about?" his pastor inquired.

"'Light as a feather' is one of those so-called parlor-room games," I explained. "Someone lies down on the floor and the others gather around the person. They put the tips of their fingers under him and chant over and over, 'You're light as a feather.' They keep doing it until they lift him in the air. Sometimes they actually hold him over their heads."

Another pastor broke in. "Are you sure it isn't just a matter of the weight distribution on their fingertips?"

I shook my head. "That's what most people think. They suppose it's some principle of physics. But I've talked to scores of people who have done this, and everyone has told me they felt no real pressure on their fingertips. The person they were lifting really did feel light as a feather."

"I remember!" Randy said. "I played it when I was five or six. . . . Yeah, I was six. My parents told me I had to stay home that night, but I sneaked out after dark. I met some of my friends in the park and someone said he had seen other kids lift a guy into the air. I thought it was a really cool thing to do. It worked."

Randy jerked. His head snapped back, then forward. "Of course it did," Disobedience said. "But even if you get rid of me, it won't do any good. I may be the gatekeeper who let all the others in, but I'm not the one who keeps all of us here. And you'll never know who he is."

"Spirit, I bind you in Jesus' name, and I command that angels hold you in torment until such time as God has revealed how we can get rid of all of you. Go down, now!"

Disobedience offered little resistance. He was convinced that we wouldn't find the clue to how he and the other demons had managed to hold Randy under their control all these years.

I asked a couple of the pastors to stay near Randy and make sure he didn't try to run away. Then I called the others aside and discussed what had happened.

"Do any of you have an idea what else he might be involved in?" I asked.

They looked at one another for some recollection. His pastor declared that Randy attended church faithfully, always got good grades in school, and never gave anyone any trouble.

"The most striking thing about him is his popularity—and his car," his pastor said.

Something quickened in me at that statement. "His car?"

"Yes, Randy is always driving up and down Main Street, showing off his car. I suppose it's not much by big-city standards, but around here it's the best car any kid has. Bright red with fancy spiked hubcaps. Randy washes it almost every day, and waxes it once a week. Yup, he's more proud of that car than any teenager I've ever seen."

"What's he like when he's not driving his car?"

Randy's pastor thought for a moment. "Now that you mention it, he's a different person. Randy's a shy boy. He comes from a poor family; he worked hard to get the car. I suppose that driving it makes him feel special."

I had heard enough. The Holy Spirit had led me to figure out how the demons maintained control over Randy, but I needed to test my theory to prove that God really had disclosed the key to Randy's deliverance.

I motioned for the pastors to follow me to the front of the church. Randy was now sitting on the pew, breathing heavily. Perspiration dripped from his brow. He grimaced and seemed to be in some kind of pain.

"Randy," I said, "if you want to be free from the demons who have you, there's only one way. You've got to give up your car."

"No! I won't do that!"

It was Randy speaking, not the demon, and I knew I had hit the most spiritually sensitive area of his life. "That car is an idol, and God will have no other gods before Him. If you want to be free, you've got to put the Lord first in your life."

"But He is," Randy argued. "What's my car got to do with it?"

"Randy, I don't want to talk to you now. Please cooperate with me. I call forth the spirit whom God has called to judgment, the spirit that controls Randy because of his car."

Randy looked at his pastor, who nodded his head. "Go on Randy. Do what Mr. Larson tells you to do."

Randy put his face in his hands. As he did, his body stiffened again, and his head pulled back. A demon manifested, but it wasn't Disobedience.

"You're the demon who has entered from Randy's obsession with his car, aren't you?"

"Maybe. What of it?"

"Do you want to be tormented like Disobedience, or are you going to cooperate?"

"I saw what you did to him. Just leave me alone. This body is mine. He wants me."

"Why? Because you help him become somebody he wouldn't be otherwise?"

"That's my function."

"And what's your name? Tell me before I call on the angels of the Lord to smite you."

"Nooooo! I'll tell you. My name is Pride."

"Are you chief among your kind?"

"Yes."

"And who is Disobedience?"

"He came in first and let the rest of us in. He's the gatekeeper. But you can't get rid of me. Randy likes me. I help him meet girls and stay popular off the football field. Because of me it doesn't matter that his parents are poor. When the two of us are in that car, he's the king of the road!"

Pride seemed calm and unperturbed, confident of his control over Randy. This story might have ended there except that God showed me what to do next.

I called Randy out of the trance and asked him to step forward with me to the altar rail at the front of the church. I told him to kneel in front of it, and I told his pastor to kneel on the other side of the rail, facing him. I asked the rest of the pastors to stand behind Randy and pray for what was about to happen.

"Do you have the keys to your car?" I asked Randy.

"Yes, in my pocket."

"Take them out and hold them in your hands."

Randy reached in his jeans and pulled out the keys. He clenched them tightly in his right fist.

"Randy, there's only one way you can be free from these demons. You have to donate your car to the church so it can be sold and the money given to missionaries. If you'll do that, give the keys to your pastor. You've got to be willing to walk the streets in humility until your pastor says you've made enough spiritual progress to drive again."

Randy tensed, but this time it wasn't the demon's reaction. His body shook almost uncontrollably, and he began sobbing. He buried his face in his hands. His right fist clenched the keys tighter and tighter.

"It's not fair! Other kids come from homes they can be proud of. Their moms and dads are important. My folks are just poor farmers. All my life the other kids made fun of me. It wasn't until I got that car that things were different."

He wept until I thought he would collapse on the floor. Then he slowly regained composure. "Mr. Larson, if you say this is what God wants me to do, I'll do it. I won't like it, but I don't want these evil things inside me anymore." Randy lowered his head in prayer. "God, forgive me. Take this pride from me. I surrender it to You."

Randy reached forward with his right arm toward his pastor. The pastor put out his hands, and Randy's fist hovered over them. Slowly Randy's hands opened. Seconds later the edge of the key chain dangled from his fingers, then a portion of the key emerged.

"Pride, I command that you attach to yourself Disobedience and all others under your control," I said. "When you leave, you will take them with you and go to the pit!"

When at last the keys fell from Randy's hand, he screamed and fell back on the floor in violent convulsions. I motioned for the pastors to stand back. The struggle we all witnessed was a battle for Randy's soul, waged over a set of car keys.

With one final hideous scream, Randy fell limp.

INNOCUOUS ACTIONS, DESTRUCTIVE DEMONS

When it comes to demonic matters, *what you don't know can hurt you*. Some sincere exorcists make the mistake of attempting deliverance on the assumption that you can only become demon possessed by deliberately committing a grievous sin. Consequently they base their approach on getting the person to confess the premeditated transgression that allowed the demons to enter. These well-meaning exorcists aren't aware that demons don't always need a volitional sin to invade someone. In fact, most of those I've met who were demon possessed had no idea they had done something that brought them into spiritual bondage.

Consider the case of Sally, a woman in her mid-twenties whom I counseled. She had a demon of hatred that caused her to self-mutilate. Her arms were covered with the scars of countless self-inflicted wounds. "I don't want to cut my body," she pleaded to me tearfully, "but I often return to consciousness from a trance to find my arms covered in blood."

What led to her desperate circumstance? One day Sally decided to read her newspaper horoscope out of curiosity. That day's prediction seemed to come true, so she began to read her astrology charts every day. Eventually, a demon of divination entered her. During the exorcism I performed on Sally, I argued with the demon about his right to possess her because of such a relatively harmless act.

"Millions of people read their horoscopes every day and never become demon possessed," I said to the demon.

The demon gave me a self-satisfied look. "You're right," the spirit agreed, "but she disobeyed what the Bible says about astrology, and that's all we needed!"

"But she wasn't a Christian. She didn't even know that the Bible condemns astrology."

"That doesn't matter! What she did let us in. We only need a sin the size of the head of a pin to enter. Give us any excuse, and we'll come in."

The fact that Sally's demon said he only needed a small sin to possess her shouldn't make us fearful that every sin of omission could lead to demonic possession. Instead, it serves as a warning to walk closely to the Lord and avoid evil at all costs. We should also pray proactively with faith, constantly seeking the Lord to keep us from temptation.

Randy became demon possessed as the result of an act of childhood curiosity, nothing more. There was no desire on his behalf to serve Satan. Though Randy's occult act wasn't intentional, he suffered the same consequence as if he had been voluntarily seeking Satan.

A naive or seemingly harmless motive is no assurance of spiritual safety. The maxim "Ignorance is no excuse for breaking the law" is as true in the spiritual realm as it is in our physical world. It does no good for a motorist to argue he didn't know what the speed limit was if the patrolman's radar gun caught him speeding. Likewise, violating God's prohibitions about entertaining the occult exacts a spiritual penalty, regardless of whether or not the offender consciously knew that he was doing wrong.

Satan seeks every advantage to overcome any resistance that our human willpower might impart. One of the best ways is by tricking people into doing things they consider spiritually innocuous. Here are a few examples. Susan was fourteen years old when she was given a Ouija board for her birthday. She thought it was just a clever game to find out the future. Andy was sixteen when he became engrossed with the game Dungeons & Dragons. He thought it was a fascinating way to use his imagination to choose characters who could cast spells. Patricia, a twelve-year-old, invited friends to her house for a slumber party where they held séances and stared at candles to talk to the dead.

Susan, Andy, and Patricia became unwitting participants in occult sins. Not one of them wanted a demon, asked for a demon, or were aware when a demon entered them. However, in a spiritual sense they were guilty and thus became open to demonic intrusion. Each of them came to me for help. Over time, through the process of several exorcisms, they were all freed.

If we humans were genuinely aware of who Satan really is and what his true motives are, none of us would toy with the occult. The evil one knows this, so he lures people into situations where they unwittingly become vulnerable to his deception through all sorts of seduction. Then Satan has them where he wants them. He makes them feel powerful, as though they are beating the spiritual odds by doing something God has forbidden without suffering any immediate negative consequences. Many consult psychics, astrologers, and fortune-tellers. They follow New Age trance channelers because they think such phenomena are spiritually harmless, and even helpful.

In Randy's case, he appeared to be innocent on two counts. First, his sin permitting demonic entry was committed while he was a child under the age of moral accountability. Second, he had no occult purpose in his actions. How could Satan possess him?

Most Christians fail to view the battle for souls as a spiritual struggle based on exacting rules of procedure, established at the dawn of creation. The devil is like a lawyer in a cosmic courtroom, arguing his case where God is the judge, eternity is at stake, and the stiffest sentence is banishment forever from the presence of God.

Unfortunately we assume that the spiritual universe functions on a basis of impartiality. If God is just, we reason, surely He won't allow a demon to take advantage of childhood innocence.

HOW THE DEVIL GOT IN MAY NOT BE HOW HE STAYS

Another lesson I learned from Randy is that the spiritual reason that allows a demon access to an individual may not be the demon's means of remaining there. Randy's demon of disobedience entered because of the "light as a feather" game. The demon stayed there because of his pride.

When a demon enters, he immediately embarks on a plan for further demonic invasion. The spirit will tempt the person to commit other sins that in turn allow other demons to enter. As the number of demons grows, they set out to dismantle the spiritual boundaries in the person. In the place of moral consciousness, the demons establish an infrastructure of evil. Like a cancer spreading from one organ to another, the spiritual malignancy extends to every vulnerable aspect of the person's spirit, soul, and body. Often the victim descends to depths of moral depravity that would have been unthinkable prior to the possession of evil spirits.

One person I met, named Larry, was an example of this. Larry grew up in a home devoid of affection from his father, and he became inordinately attached to his mother. His obsessive anger toward his father eventually allowed a demon of rebellion to enter him. Once inside Larry, Rebellion recognized his victim's emotional condition as the perfect setup for a companion spirit of homosexuality. Larry's homosexual lifestyle wasn't the original reason he became possessed; it was the by-product of a long history of internal spiritual decline.

Larry's story makes this point: The counselor seeking to free one from demons should always look for the root sin that led to the initial possession. It may not be obvious. Focusing on other demons that manifest more violent and offensive behavior may be concentrating on a symptom of the victim's spiritual condition rather than its foundational cause. As in Randy's case, both the sin of original entry of Rebellion and the emotional factors that allowed Homosexuality to control him needed to be addressed before Larry was free.

DELIVERANCE

Many people have strange ideas about deliverance from demons. Hollywood and horror books evoke images of a minister in a clerical collar, waving a crucifix and slinging holy water. Those involved are usually depicted as fearful and hysterical. The victim is generally caricatured as hideous and insane, spitting green pea soup and vaulting about the room as if he were catapulted on a supernatural trampoline. The final stage of the struggle is seen as a conflict between the exorcist and the demon.

This fictitious portrayal hides one of the devil's best kept secrets: The real battle is between the demon and the victim's will. The exorcist is a representative of God, just coaching the proceedings. He may guide the steps of the procedure, but the decisive contest is based on the victim asserting his will to be free. This can be accomplished by the victim's verbal confession of repentance, followed by his spoken command for the demon to leave.

Casting Out a Demon by an Act of Self-Deliverance

My use of the term *self-deliverance* has no relationship to the abhorrent use of these words by euthanasia advocates as a euphemism for suicide. I'm referring to a process of deliverance that requires less involvement by the principal exorcist. The victim's spiritual growth is sufficient to resist Satan, and all he needs is prayerful assistance and minimal instruction.

The number of victims able to achieve self-deliverance is small. This rare occurrence takes place when weak demons hang on for some undetected reason. The victim, meanwhile, grows spiritually in God's grace. All that's left to accomplish spiritual wholeness is a final expulsion of minor demonic intruders. Deliverance may come without the victim even knowing it immediately, but definite changes will result.

Roberta had been victimized by a satanic cult and came to me for help. I ministered to her for several months and performed at least a dozen exorcisms. All the evil spirits were driven out, except for a small circle of demons that functioned to make Roberta spiritually insecure. Whenever I tried to cast them out, they claimed the right of Roberta's failure to fully trust in her position as a believer.

I spent many hours going through the Scriptures, reminding Roberta of who she was in Christ. I pointed out that the power of Christ's resurrection had raised her spiritually so that she was made to sit in the heavenly places in Christ Jesus (Eph. 2:6). I emphasized Roberta's completeness in Jesus, according to Colossians 2:10. I also encouraged her to believe she could do anything through Christ (Phil. 4:13) and asked her to exert her authority as a believer (Luke 10:19) to stand up to the devil (James 4:7).

Roberta took these lessons to heart and applied them every day. I didn't see her for nearly a year, and when I met with her again, she asked me to see if any spirits were present. Carefully I went through every testing procedure I knew that would arouse and detect demons. From all I could tell at that moment, all the demons were gone.

"I knew it in my heart," Roberta told me, "but it made me feel better to confirm it." Then she explained something peculiar. "I was in church one Sunday morning. I think it was during the time we sing praise choruses. I suddenly felt a sick feeling in my stomach. For a moment I thought I was going to throw up. Then, whatever was in my stomach rose through my chest and into my mouth. The nausea subsided and I yawned. It was a most unusual yawn—not like when one is sleepy. It was as if I had to open my mouth and let something out. At that instant I knew I had gotten rid of those demons."

She went on. "There was a momentary, stabbing pain in my throat and it was over. I know this sounds strange, but I felt as if a ton of weight left my body. In fact, when I got home from church I got out my bathroom scale to see if I'd lost any pounds. I hadn't, of course, but the sensation of weight loss was so real I had to check."

Not every victim of demon possession can be as spiritually successful as Roberta, nor will they experience the same things in the process of relief. Yet, I believe more people could be freed if those who seek to deliver them would take the time to minister God's Word effectively. Self-deliverance can be a reality, but it takes time and patience. The benefit is that those who have been self-delivered have a greater possibility of keeping their freedom, because they are less likely to fall back into the same sins that held them in bondage.

Casting Out a Demon by Modified Self-Deliverance

Randy was an example of what I call modified self-deliverance. When the final victory came, it wasn't necessary for me to engage in a lengthy dialogue with the demons to verbally command their departure. I did have to tell Randy what to do, and those gathered with us interceded in prayer to create an atmosphere of faith that weakened the evil spirits. When Randy dropped those keys into his pastor's hands, it was the unspoken equivalent of an oral rebuke, denying the demons inside him any further right to stay.

Modified self-deliverance is an approach that involves the will and verbal stand of the victim. It may entail leading the victim in specific prayers, and encouraging the person to make confessional decisions that will break the hold of certain sins. The reward is seeing the one victimized by the devil exercise moral fortitude to claim his own freedom in the name of Jesus!

Demonic Hindrances to Deliverance

Most victims of demons are unable to do what Randy did. The spirits' hold is so strong that any attempt by the victim to resist them is met with a severe counterattack. There are several common methods used by demons. One is putting the person into a demonic trance. In this condition a demon manifests and dominates the victim's consciousness so he or she cannot speak or think. Demons also employ distraction techniques such as mental fogging to diminish clarity of thought or the infliction of intense pain, which breaks the victim's concentration.

Certain demons actually go by the name Blocker, which also describes their function. I have dealt with hundreds of demons like this. They belong to a category of evil spirits whose sole purpose is to hinder the progress of the exorcism. They may make the person mute, so he cannot respond to inquiries or pray against the demons. Other blockers will make the victim temporarily blind, which creates a terrifying experience. One blocker I encountered induced a condition of paralysis.

Some demons can produce a comatose state. I have actually dealt with a blocker demon that went by the name Coma. He was not the most powerful demon, but he had a crucial function. In fact, I was unable to deal with any other demon as long as he was around. Whenever I tried to confront a demon in this system, Coma would manifest and literally place the victim in a comatose state.

Once when Coma took over, a medical physician confirmed the true comatose condition. This tactic not only blocked my access to the chief demons I needed to cast out, it also delayed my ability to help. The demon knew the limitations of my busy schedule and would taunt me by threatening to black out his victim and waste what time I did have.

The casting out of Coma came under most unusual circumstances. In the midst of profound frustration, God reminded me of the account in 1 Kings 17, when Elijah revived the widow's son. First Kings 17:17 says the son was so sick "there was no breath left in him." Apparently, he had entered some kind of death state, perhaps a comatose condition. The

Bible says Elijah "stretched himself out on the child three times" and prayed. Then "the soul of the child came back to him, and he revived" (v. 22).

During the exorcism of Coma, I asked the two ministers who were assisting me, "This may sound bizarre, but I want you to pray earnestly while I stretch myself out over this man three times, just like Elijah did. Help me lay him on the floor, and I'll hold myself up by my fingers and toes over his body. By faith let's believe that our trust in God's Word is going to defeat Coma."

When I stood to my feet after the third time, Coma manifested in a state of rage. I knew by his fury that his right to continue inducing comatose states had been broken, and he was promptly cast out. We were then able to move on to deal with the more important demons who were there by spiritual rights. We had overcome the forces of evil.

The Joy of Freedom

That spring afternoon in the rural Canadian community Randy claimed such freedom. After he gave those car keys to his pastor, the pastor knelt by Randy's side and prayed softly. "Lord, fill Randy with Your Holy Spirit and make him more of a man than he ever was. Whatever that car meant to him, I ask You to be that and more to him. In place of the pride of Satan, place a humble spirit in his heart that will make him love You more than all the possessions in this world."

It was a benediction to a battle this rural Canadian community wouldn't soon forget. A son in their city had been set free.

CHAPTER 6

What the Devil Can't Do to You

Maria, a sixteen-year-old teenager, left a lasting impression on me. She wore Coke bottle–sized eyeglasses because she was legally blind, and even with those glasses she could only make out shadowy images. She approached me after a church service to ask some questions about her spiritual condition.

As we began talking about some of the problems in her life, the demonic spirit came forth and verbally challenged me. I called for the pastor who led us into his office where we were soon joined by Maria's father.

I was pleased her father could be involved in the experience. Whenever I am dealing with a minor, I always try to include the parents. This serves two purposes. First, it enhances the follow-up because the parents understand more clearly how their child became subjected to evil forces, so they know how to pray for and spiritually encourage their child. Second, parents have a God-given authority to rebuke a demon, which may have greater effectiveness than that of an experienced exorcist.

The extraordinary thing about Maria's demon was the way he expressed himself. He would move Maria's right arm slowly toward her face, grasp her glasses, and take them off. Because he didn't need glasses, he could not see through the heavy lenses.

In fact, the first time the spirit manifested, he spoke with disgust. "I hate these things," he said, pointing to the glasses. "I can't see a thing when she has them on."

"You don't need them to see?" I asked.

"Of course not," the spirit replied, insulted by my question. "It's the only thing I hate about being in this body. I have to put up with her eyesight!"

I reached for a nearby Bible, randomly selected a page, and laid the text on Maria's lap. "Read this," I said.

"Well, I hate reading *that* book, but if it's all you've got . . ." The spirit rolled his eyes in exasperation and proceeded to read the entire page. He paused every few seconds and looked up with a smirk, as if he were pleased to demonstrate that he wasn't limited by Maria's eyesight. Under his control, Maria's eyes functioned with 20/20 vision!

Normally a demon detests the Word of God, but this demon was so proud of his ability to see through Maria's eyes, he somehow overcame his revulsion to Scripture.

Maria's case raises important questions. Can an evil spirit overtake the faculties of a victim and manifest his presence in place of their neurosensory responses? Just what can Satan do, and what can't he do?

WHAT THE DEVIL *CANNOT* DO

Can Demons Invade the Spirit of a Christian?

When I first became involved in exorcisms, I assumed that a Christian was immune from the torment of demons. I based that assumption on the influence of other Christian leaders who convinced me of this. I had perfected the logic explaining my position: "The Holy Spirit and an evil spirit can't dwell in the same vessel." "Light and darkness cannot coexist." "Those who cast demons out of Christians are making excuses for sin problems."

I had even given messages to large audiences, boldly declaring that the very idea of a Christian having a demon was heresy. I insisted that Christians claiming to have demons were making excuses for problems of carnality or personal lack of discipline; they were avoiding the tough part of growing in grace and maturing in a deeper understanding of Scripture.

I overcame this theological prejudice when I agreed to pray with a woman named Audrey. She claimed to be a Christian, but said she had demons. I thought perhaps Audrey wasn't sure what it meant to be a Christian. During our discussion several demons manifested. One was a spirit of death. It overtook her, and she looked as though she were comatose. She was lying rigidly on the floor with her hands stiff against her sides. A pastor and I tried to make her as comfortable as possible. We watched to make sure she was breathing. Her pulse slowed until she only wheezed small spurts of breath. I believed that she was going to die if we didn't intervene.

For several hours we maintained a vigil of prayer until Audrey's pulse and breathing were restored and she regained consciousness. I was puzzled. How could a Christian have a demon and be pushed to the point of death? I wasn't sure how to pray for her because I was confused that darkness and light could dwell together.

After Audrey regained consciousness I interrogated the demon. "What part of her do you possess?"

"I don't have her spirit, that belongs to God. But I do have her body. I entered into her before she became a Christian, when she was involved in the occult."

The demon spat, growled, and taunted me, knowing I was unsure of myself. But I took control with the authority of Christ and within two hours I had cast out Death and the other spirits who entered with him. Audrey rededicated her life to Christ and has never again been affected by this life-threatening spirit.

After that experience I began searching the Word of God more diligently about the matter of demons influencing Christians. I discovered that the issue wasn't as conclusive as I had thought. Gradually I understood that my error was based on a narrow understanding of demonic phenomena, and a predetermined reading of Scripture. In my honest moments of contemplation, I realized that those pastors and Bible teachers who had repeatedly reinforced the "Christian can't have a demon" outlook had very little practical experience with the phenomenon. I concluded that, while doctrine is not based on experience, the lack of experiential testimony about such a crucial area of spiritual deliverance was a glaring weakness.

As I began to discuss the subject with others, I learned that theological sentiments are often based on extreme examples. Almost everyone opposed to the idea of Christians having a demon could relate one or more horrific stories about exorcism sessions in which Christians were encouraged to think of their spiritual failures as having a demonic root. They were then told to vomit up demons of everything from morning sickness to nasal congestion—seriously! I had witnessed some of these deliverance sessions. Highly manipulative evangelists preyed on distraught and gullible people who were looking for a quick solution to their spiritual and physical misery.

I have since learned the simple truth that when you belong to God, what Satan cannot invade is your *spirit*. The moment a person is born into the kingdom of God by faith in Christ (Eph. 2:8–9), the spirit is eternally reborn and belongs to God. Jesus declared in John 10:28 that no one has the power to "snatch" us out of God's hand. However, man is a tripartite being (1 Thess. 5:23), and there are aspects of the human condition that Satan *can* afflict. While he is prohibited from touching the spirit of God's saints, nothing prevents him from tormenting the body and soul—if the disobedient conduct of a Christian allows him to do so.

Much confusion about this issue exists because of the use of the word *possession*. The term doesn't appear in the original Greek language of the New Testament. Bible scholars say those who translated the King James edition added this word in order to classify varying degrees of demonic control. More correctly, the words translated "possession" should simply be rendered "demonized," that is, under the influence of a demon. Attempting to be verbally precise about such a supernatural phenomenon is pointless. You can't take something enshrouded in a mystical context and reduce it to a paradigm of human language. That's why we must cautiously use terms associated with demons.

I do use words like *possession, oppression,* and *obsession* to describe varying degrees of control. By *possession* I mean that the spirit is internalized and claims certain legal rights to invade the person's body. Demonic "possession" never means a Christian's regenerated spirit has been invaded or that the demon owns the human being. It means that his or her soul or body is influenced by a demon. The demon can manifest through the host's faculties—that is, see with the eyes, speak through the vocal cords, and even subject the person to a trance state of mental oblivion. Deliverance comes when the demon inside is cast outside.

Oppression occurs when a demon has not entered the victim and cannot manifest through the victim's neurosensory system. It's as if the spirit were sitting on the person's shoulder, constantly harassing him or her, trying to push all the right buttons to make the person do his bidding.

Obsession describes a condition of slightly less control. The spirit can't influence his victim quite as easily as with oppression, but his leverage still exceeds that of "normal" temptations and urges. In both oppression and obsession, freedom comes, not by exorcism, but by a binding of the demon, subjecting it to restraint by a command in Christ's authority.

What about those instances in which a demon manifests in a Christian? In most cases the demon entered before the believer's conversion to Christianity, and the evil spirit continued to control some part of the person's life because the specific occult sin was never renounced. The demon claims squatter's rights.

The metaphor of what happens when territory is conquered in a war applies here. Even though the conflict may be officially ended, enemy snipers refuse to surrender, so they must be hunted down. Their right to remain may be technically voided since the territory is under new control, but that doesn't mean they leave automatically or give up easily. An offense must be mounted to enforce the terms of victory. The exorcist must diligently pursue every avenue of deliverance to be certain that every demonic influence has been conquered.

In this book I have used the term *legal right* with a very specific definition. I am not referring to any spiritually lawful power over a Christian's spirit that a demon may claim. The cross of Christ has cancelled Satan's legal rights to the believer. Evil spirits that demonize Christians are invaders, intruding where they do not belong; they have no authority to remain. By legal I mean a spiritual technicality whereby demons argue the letter of the law, presuming that their resistance is legitimate. In a certain sense, their claim is more literally *moral* than *legal*. However, because of the sense of exacting assertion suggested by the word *legal*, I am using it as a way to emphasize the lawyerly manner in which the exorcist must approach whatever claims on the victim the demon may illegitimately avow.

Can Demons Force Their Will upon You?

Those unacquainted with spiritual warfare may assume that demonic "possession" reduces victims to a zombielike state. In this condition, they are slaves to whatever the demon desires. This is not the case.

Satan cannot force his will upon anyone. His only power is the power of persuasion. Even in the worst cases of demonic possession, the evil spirits never totally control the wills of their victims at all times. I once dealt with a man who had committed murder in the name of Satan. In spite of his morally degenerate condition, he had lucid spiritual moments when we had profound discussions about the condition of his soul. Eventually he was able to call upon the Lord for salvation. After this, the demons were cast out easily because he had forcefully exercised his will against them.

In another situation a woman had ascended to the highest ranks of black magic in a satanic cult. To ensure her status she had committed heinous atrocities and had even consented to the human sacrifice of her best friend in order to save her own life.

In the beginning of my dealings with her, spirits would immediately place her in a trance whenever the name of Christ was mentioned. Sometimes it took hours of prayer and fasting to bring her out of the trance. She often lost days at a time when she had no recollection of where she had been or what she had done.

Yet there was a small part of her that Satan was unable to completely overpower. That part grew stronger and stronger as she spent time in prayer and God's Word. Bit by bit, she overcame the darkness with Light, and was able to have lengthier conversations about spiritual matters. After months of encouragement, she completed a prayer of commitment to Christ.

I always tell those bound by demons to call upon that small portion of their will that is not dominated by the devil. In every case, if the victim truly wanted to withstand Satan's power, he or she was able to do so. No matter how evil a person has been, God sovereignly preserves a part of the person's soul. When they respond to God's truth, they are freed from bondage.

Can Demons Physically Afflict a Christian?

To answer the question of whether a Christian can be physically afflicted, we must first explore the means by which demons influence Christians.

Do Christians sin? Of course. First John 1:8–9 says we do. We cannot continue to abide in sin because of the indwelling nature of Christ. Note, however, that in Ephesians 4:23 Christians are admonished to "be renewed in the spirit of your mind." If the mind of the Christian needs renewal, then it stands to reason that when our minds are not renewed, they may be, to some degree, under the control of ungodly forces.

"Present your bodies a living sacrifice," we read in Romans 12:1. This means our bodies may not be completely sacrificed to God, and could therefore be influenced by Satan. The lack of spirituality in the life of a Christian doesn't necessarily mean he or she is possessed. But it does mean that some part of the Christian's nature is open to evil forces.

In Luke 13:16, Christ cast a demon out of a "daughter of Abraham." It's true she wasn't living under the covenant of grace this side of the cross, but as an Old Testament devotee of God she was spiritually protected by the best that God could offer that side of Calvary. Yet a spirit of physical infirmity demonized her.

In fact, the first demon that Jesus cast out came from an apparently devout Jew in the synagogue on the Sabbath. Christ's first exorcism was in a church! That man in Luke 4:33–35 was certainly "possessed," because the demon spoke through his body. Christ told the unclean spirit to "come out of him" (v. 35).

Can Satan Take Your Life?

In spite of all that God allowed Job to suffer at the hands of the devil, the Lord drew the line at Job's life. ("Behold, he is in your hand, but spare his life" [Job 2:6].) I have had my own life threatened many times by demons. They have repeatedly told me that my intervention to free souls from Satan would cost me my life. Once it almost did.

During an exorcism, an individual in a demonic trance materialized a knife and pointed it at my throat. (I recognized the knife as the one I kept in a drawer in my office, fifteen miles away! This person hadn't been to my office, and certainly wouldn't have known where the knife was kept.)

I stood motionless as the sharp point of the blade pressed against the skin at my neck and was poised to pierce my Adam's apple. A momentary thrust forward with the blade would have ended my life. There was no question in my mind that the demon fully intended to slit my throat.

Others who were there to assist in the exorcism could not come to my aid because they were afraid the person would kill me. They silently prayed for God's intervention on my behalf, but they stood perfectly still.

The demon pushed me toward a wall until my back was flat against it, with nowhere to turn. "Where is your God now?" the spirit taunted me. "I'm going to kill you and prove that your God isn't as powerful as you say He is. If God is all you claim He is, I wouldn't have this knife at your throat!"

In that moment, as I faced certain death at the hands of a demon, a supernatural composure came over me. "I don't know if God will let you kill me," I responded, "but I do know this. If God allows you to cut my throat, you will. If He doesn't, you won't. Whether or not you kill me is in God's hands, not yours."

The demon's eyes flared ever brighter. He seemed furious that I wasn't pleading for my life.

"We can make a deal," he offered. "I'll spare your life if you back off and leave us alone."

The spirit slowly twisted the point of the blade, and I felt it bore slightly into my skin, piercing the flesh. If I have ever been tempted to reach an accommodation with a demon, that was it. But I knew better. Many people had cautioned me about dealing with demons, fearful my life would be endangered. I had always told them, "The safest place in the world is in the center of God's will. That is the one place where the devil can't harm you." Now my faith in God's Word and His protection was being put to the test.

I have no idea how long I stood immobilized. I suppose it was seconds, though it felt like hours. Beads of perspiration formed on my brow as I quietly prayed. I felt the hands of the demon-possessed person begin to shake, and I wondered if the unsteady way he held the knife might cause him to injure me even if he didn't kill me. I thought of trying to call the person out of the trance, but I determined that even if I was successful, the shock he would experience could thrust his arm forward.

My mind raced. *What if he falls off balance? Suppose he hears a noise or something startles him and his arm jerks forward?*

In the midst of my speculation, unseen hands seemed to restrain the arm of the demon and then pull him backward. As the knife withdrew, I let out a deep sigh. The person suddenly returned from the demonic trance, horrified to find he was holding a knife to my throat. Slowly he stepped back and lowered his arm. I quickly grabbed his wrist and forced the knife to the ground.

God did not allow my life to be taken, but He permitted me to reach the brink of death. My faith was tested to the limit. At that moment I learned that faith isn't a presumptuous conclusion about what we hope God will or will not allow. Rather it is a quiet trust that no matter what God permits the devil to do, He is in ultimate control.

I didn't die that day because my life was in the Lord's hands. The day of my departure from this earthly vessel is appointed by Him. No demon can usurp that authority. When we walk in God's will and seek to acknowledge Him in all our ways, He directs our path. If I had died at the hands of that demon, it wouldn't have been because the demon outsmarted or overwhelmed the Holy Spirit. It would have been because God, in some mysterious way, had chosen to call me home in that fashion.

In almost every exorcism I have conducted, the demons have threatened to kill their victims. Often this threat is made to intimidate the exorcist, in hope the fear of such a tragedy will make him back away. Yet, in the hundreds of exorcisms in which I have been involved, I have never known a victim of demons to be killed or permanently harmed. Just the opposite usually occurs. The threats of the demons have proven to be hollow in the presence of God's glory.

WHAT THE DEVIL *CAN* DO

Satan Can Deliver the Goods

Satan's powers of temptation are his most irresistible lure, and he isn't always bluffing. Many times he can fulfill what he pledges. In Matthew, chapter 4, Jesus didn't dispute the tempter's claims of worldly domination. Satan offered Jesus all the kingdoms of this world, and Christ tacitly acknowledged the devil's ability to fulfil that bid.

I've known people possessed by demons who supplied them with drugs, sex, money, and a host of other evils. "Serve me," Satan said, "and all this will be yours." They served him, and he delivered. But that delivery was for a moment and for a huge price. No sinful satisfaction is forever, and the cost is immeasurable. What Lucifer offers in one realm, he extracts at a horrible price in another. People will make compromises with their souls for the most base of reasons.

For example, Marlene was a victim of multiple sclerosis and was confined to a wheelchair. She wanted to walk, but her disease left her unable to control most of her muscles. In desperation she called on the devil. "If God won't heal me, Satan can have my life!" she declared in a fit of rage one day.

Her proposition gave demons the right to possess her. One night I watched her, under demonic control, get out of her wheel chair, walk across a room, and attack two men who were praying for her freedom. While this was happening, she was aware enough to realize Satan had partially made good on his bargain. The devil allowed her to walk—at the price of possession.

We struggled for hours to convince Marlene she had to fully renounce her pact with Lucifer. Part of her wanted to, but another part was gratified that the demons made her muscles capable of doing what they couldn't do naturally. Eventually, I stopped the exorcism because Marlene was not cooperating fully, and I determined we were wasting our time. Victims of possession can only be freed if they truly want liberation at any cost. Any unwillingness to relinquish a benefit the demon appears to give, will be a foothold for the demon to continue his activities.

I've prayed for Marlene since then, and I hope she's been freed; but I've never forgotten that she was willing to spend an eternity in hell in exchange for a few moments of walking.

Not everyone's situation is as dramatic as Marlene's. I have known cases of possession in which Satan bargained with people who were timid and offered them an extroverted personality. Others who had been rejected found acceptance in a satanic cult. Or physically unattractive people have suddenly found themselves desired by cult members. But in every case, the trade-off was at a terrible consequence.

Satan cannot truly give what he promises. And he can't make people accept the terms of his contract. He can only allure with assurances of the forbidden. On occasion, one may taste the fruit of his temptation, as Eve did, but the satisfaction will not be lasting.

Satan Can Control a Christian's Thoughts and Words

Let me explain how Satan can also control the thoughts and speech of a Christian. In Matthew, chapter 16, Jesus had just concluded His explanation to His disciples on the true nature of His earthly mission—that He must suffer and die (v. 21). Peter immediately spoke up in an effort to dissuade Christ from going to the cross: "Far be it from You, Lord; this shall not happen to You!" (v. 22).

The response of Christ was abrupt and stern. "Get behind Me, Satan!" Jesus said *to Peter* (v. 23). I'm not suggesting that Peter was demon possessed. I am proposing that Peter, while standing in the presence of Christ, was sufficiently influenced that he literally spoke the words Satan wanted him to say. Even more astounding is the fact that earlier in verse 16 of that chapter, Peter had given the confessional statement of faith on which Christ said He would build His church!

In Acts, chapter 5, Ananias and Sapphira, members of the early church, lied to the apostle Peter. They had sold some possessions to give to the church, then had second thoughts and conspired to keep back a portion for themselves. When Peter asked them what amount they had received for the sale, Ananias and Sapphira lied. What was the source of that lie? The apostle Peter said, "Satan filled your heart to lie to the Holy Spirit" (v. 3) In judgment, God struck them dead. If we accept the assumption that Ananias and Sapphira experienced the new birth in Christ, then how can we explain away the fact that their hearts were filled by Satan to such an extent, they were capable of committing a sin worthy of such abrupt and severe divine judgment?

Satan can, in some instances, take over a Christian's mind and speak through his lips. Demons are in certain instances able to place Christians in a trance state so that the unclean spirit controls psychomotor functions and conscious mental processes. I have dealt with scores of cases of people who were undeniably followers of Christ, and yet demons spoke through them and even violently attacked me. It is disingenuous to suggest that they somehow lost their salvation long enough to let a demon in and then thereafter resumed their Christian walk.

If Satan can control our speech when we are disobedient and fill our hearts with evil when we are rebellious, he may be able to do a lot more to Christians than we would like to admit. What scriptural lessons can we learn from this startling information?

A Christian can be born again and have spiritual victory over the original Adamic sin that eternally separates mankind from God and still have besetting sins (Heb. 12:1)—uncontrolled thoughts, resentment, anger, and bitterness. Salvation must not be confused with sanctification. The Holy Spirit's continuing work of grace is a progressive act of God's desire to draw us closer to Him.

Those who, yet saved, resist this scriptural plea (1 Thess. 4:3) may find they have harbored demonic pockets of activity from their pre-conversion lives. This message needs a greater emphasis in our churches so that we may set free any of our brothers and sisters in Christ who are suffering the "hangover" of Satan's influence from their former lives of sin.

As kindly as I can say it, those who underestimate what Christians can suffer at the hand of Satan are doing a disservice to the body of Christ. They are consigning sincere Christians to a life of continued demonic influence and causing needless suffering in the lives of those whom the Lord would set free.

Let no one misunderstand me. A Christian cannot be demonized if by "possession" you mean "ownership." The child of God is owned by the Lord. But I will testify that a Christian can be severely influenced by demons and even be inhabited by them. I will also do all that I can in Jesus' name to see that those who are "heirs of God and joint heirs with Christ" (Rom. 8:17) will experience the hope of freedom from demonic bondage.

CHAPTER 7

✝ *Satan Doesn't Play Fair*

According to a recent *USA Today* report, today's runaways are different from a generation ago. The youngsters who hit today's mean streets aren't there because they don't want to go home. Some are afraid to go home, where abusive parents and stepparents sexually molest them. Some have been told to hit the road because one of the parents simply didn't want them anymore. They were either a drain on the family's financial resources or an interference with a parent's lifestyle. Tony's tale is the story of how evil seeks to devour this generation of youth, and how Satan exploits their emotional pain to lure them into indulging in occult ceremonies.

I first became aware of nineteen-year-old Tony through a letter he wrote to me. One page was filled with elaborately detailed pencil drawings of me in various stages of torture and dismemberment. These depictions were accompanied by line illustrations of satanic symbols: a baphomet (goat's head pentagram), a dagger dripping with blood, a hooded figure with a scythe, and a mutilated Christ figure hanging upside down on a cross.

Another page was covered with the names of death metal bands like Slayer, Danzig, Venom, and Dark Angel. Tony had also scribbled slogans borrowed from the lexicon of lyrics by these bands, including: "All the Holy Divers shall kneel to Satan" (from a Dio album) and "Spill the blood and let it run onto me" (from a Slayer album).

Tony also inscribed his own aphorisms: "Death to all Christ followers." "I promise to kill my father." "They have taken my soul and suicide is the only solution." And "Hail Satan." Below all of these statements were contradictory but desperate cries for help. Finally in closing, below the words, "Your dead friend, Tony," he wrote, "Help me, I beg you."

A secular psychiatrist might have had a field day analyzing the convoluted and threatening way Tony expressed himself. I saw a plain pattern of rejection and a profound sense of worthlessness.

I prayed earnestly and then answered Tony's letter. That led to a series of phone conversations. A demon manifested during a few phone calls and spoke to me. On one occasion an unidentified spirit made a chilling boast: "Tony made a pact with me when he mingled the blood of animals and children. That gave me full rights to him!"

The fact that I was able to correspond with Tony and talk with him on the phone raises the question: "Why couldn't Tony's demons prevent this from happening?" Couldn't they have overtaken him to prevent him from reaching out for help?

WHERE DO DEMONS RESIDE?

Some people don't understand where demons abide when they aren't actively controlling their victim. Possession isn't a static phenomenon. The person who has a demon may not have that particular demon all the time. If the host is a willing recipient of unclean spirits, and has an open door of access, demons can come and go at will. They don't have to stay in the victim permanently. Satan is not omnipresent; he is limited in his ability to be anywhere he wants anytime he wants.

I've encountered situations where demons, previously identified as possessing the host, were not there at some point in the exorcism. Other spirits in the host acknowledged that the missing demons were outside on another mission. In that case I was able to "lock out" the absent demons and keep them from returning.

Exorcisms are often complex procedures and need to be performed methodically, sometimes over an extended period of time. Not doing so may preclude the opportunity to face an important demon. For example, in one case a demon that was critical to the domination of the victim was absent during the early stages of the exorcism. If I had ended the procedure prematurely, I would never have known about this spirit, and he would have come back later. (I couldn't "lock" him out, since I didn't know about him.) This may explain why some who minister deliverance discover that a person they thought was totally freed once again has demons they never knew about. To keep this from happening, we might ask the Lord to forbid reentrance of spirits who exited without going to the pit.

MEETING TONY FACE-TO-FACE

I became very concerned about Tony and suggested that I fly into his city for a confrontation with his demons. I arrived a few days later and met Tony, who was accompanied by the pastor of a church he had attended. Tony was short, stocky, and dressed in a leather jacket, black jeans, and a black T-shirt with the logo of a death metal band, and the slogan "Evil Knows No Boundaries." His head was shaved, except for a punk-style strip down the middle. Silver rings were inserted through three holes in each earlobe.

When he saw me, Tony pulled the lapel of his black motorcycle coat over his face and hid behind it. It took hours of talking before he would sit up straight in his chair and look me in the eye. He was a teenager who believed nobody wanted him—nobody but the devil.

Whenever I tried to talk to Tony his demons came forth and challenged me. After discussing the situation with his pastor, we decided there was no choice but to attempt an exorcism. For four days Tony's pastor and I battled dozens of demons, casting them out one by one.

The pastor was a man of faith and stood shoulder-to-shoulder with me throughout the battle. He had heard about cases of demon possession and preached about demons and the devil, but he had never encountered anything like this. Without him, the struggle for Tony's soul would have failed. Even when he didn't understand why I was taking a particular direction during the deliverance, Tony's pastor gave me his full confidence and prayed unceasingly.

The final struggle was with a spirit who called himself Christ. Whenever he manifested, Tony's right arm shot straight out, stiffened like a "Seig Heil" salute, and his hands formed the sign of Satan (fist clenched except for the first and little fingers extended).

I recognized this as the spirit who had threatened me over the phone. He claimed to have entered when Tony's coven sacrificed an eight-year-old child who had been kidnapped from a playground! "We crucified that child like we did your Jesus," the demon declared. "We pierced the child's hands and ripped open his side." The ghastly deed had been prefaced by the sacrifice of a pig. As a finale, the blood of the two were mixed.

I must pause from Tony's story for a moment to deal with a crucial issue regarding human misunderstandings about what Satan is allowed to do. Certainly the kidnapping and murder of an innocent child doesn't seem "fair." Is Satan obligated to abide by human standards of what seems acceptable?

DOES SATAN ABIDE BY HUMAN STANDARDS?

I recall facing a demon that had possessed a woman since she was five years old. At the time, an elderly male cult member sexually molested her in a deliberate attempt to pass on his spirits to continue the cult heritage.

"What you've done isn't fair!" I protested.

"Fair?" the demon retorted. "Who said that we demons play fair. Fairness is a human ideal you get from your God. To us there are no rules. We do whatever we can to possess a body. You underestimate what we can do, because you can't imagine anything as bad as we are. Why do you think the world is as depraved and violent as it is?"

Demons are dirty fighters. A fallen spirit has no illusions about maintaining some sense of propriety. The only restraint on an unclean spirit is the presence of God's Spirit dwelling in His people and the offensive posture taken by Christians who wage spiritual war against the forces of darkness. Prayer is a powerful weapon in our fight against these principalities.

Hearing about the abduction and murder of a child concerned the pastor and me. We questioned Tony in detail about what happened. He said he wasn't the one who actually got the child, and he claimed he was only an observer of the crucifixion; there was no way he knew exactly who was responsible for the crimes. We encouraged Tony to go to the authorities, though we discovered later that the police showed no interest in Tony's story. Since occult crime is seldom a focus of law enforcement agencies, the criminal activities of satanic cults are not often detected and even less frequently investigated.

IS HUMAN SACRIFICE PRACTICED TODAY BY SATANIC CULTS?

Though our society would prefer to ignore the reality of human sacrifice, such unthinkable acts to appease occult powers have a well-established history in many ancient cultures. The Mayas, Aztecs, and Incas of Central and South America elevated the practice to such levels of horror that the Spanish conquistadors were able to use this barbarousness as an excuse for genocide. (On special occasions, the pagan priests killed thousands in a single day to ensure the cycles of seasons.) Even today, archaeologists continue to excavate 500-year-old bodies from the icy slopes of the Andean mountains. If the priest did not perform this bloody ritual, these people believed the sun would cease its path through the heavens; therefore the victims of these ritual offerings often went to their fate willingly, considering their death to be honorable. They relished the moment when the Aztec or Incan priest would plunge an obsidian knife into their chests, because they were a propitiation for the entire civilization.

Historical revisionists have made a high-minded attempt to avoid sensationalizing such embarrassing spectacles. To admit that such butchery existed would concede the rationale for missionaries to convert these pagan systems. Even today, in remote sections of Peru and Bolivia where I have visited, consistent rumors insist that the descendants of these primitive priests clandestinely practice the old ways during the outbreak of natural disasters, serious illness, famine, and extreme weather conditions; they believe that the shedding of human blood is the only way to pacify the forces of the mountains and the skies.

The ancients sacrificed to achieve something they needed, such as rain, bountiful crops, or sexual fertility. They also sought to appease the gods they feared. Certain tribes invoked the deities' assistance against an enemy in times of war. Some sacrifices were performed to authenticate devotion or emphasize worthiness.

Contemporary cults use human sacrifice for many different reasons. Devout satanists believe they must break all of God's Ten Commandments, especially the sixth. They leave murder as their grand finale, the ultimate act of allegiance. Other cults systematically use sacrificial murder to fearfully bind members to the cult. On occasion, Satan will manifest himself in some way and call for a human sacrifice to appease his lust for blood, proving he has been "a murderer from the beginning" (John 8:44).

As was the case with Tony's cult, victims of modern devil worshipers are often obtained by kidnapping unattended children, as well as throwaway and runaway kids. In some cults, female breeders are kept to deliver babies for whom there is no record of birth or death. Some cult members consider it a privilege to bear a baby for slaughter.

"Where are the bodies?" the critics cry. Some are burned in ceremonial fires, and the ashes scattered. Satanists may infiltrate a crematorium staff and use the ovens unnoticed. Garbage disposal sites, abandoned mine shafts, and remote lakes serve as dumping places. Other bodies are eaten by acids or ground up in tree-eating machinery. To those still unconvinced that human sacrifice cults can elude authorities, I challenge, "Bring me the body of Jimmy Hoffa." If organized crime could kill a notable person like Hoffa, escape the most intensive of investigations, and leave no trace of his body, why couldn't satanic cults aided by supernatural evil forces do the same?

UNDERSTANDING THE UNPARDONABLE SIN

After we spent several hours praying with Tony about what he had done, we led him in prayers of repentance. Then we proceeded to deal with the demon who called himself Christ. A curious aspect of this exorcism was the physical way the demon enforced his right.

"Tony is mine, he bears my seal," the spirit shouted over and over. When I rebuked that claim, the Christ demon became furious and expressed his legal right even more vehemently. Finally the demon screamed, "Tony is branded forever. He'll never belong to your God."

I called Tony out of the trance. "Have you ever been branded in any way?" I asked.

Tony looked exhausted and his eyes were downcast. He pulled up the right sleeve of his shirt, and with his left hand, pointed to his forearm. Carved into his flesh was a scar with the numbers 666. "Yeah, I did this when they appointed me high priest of the coven." Tony wept out of hopelessness. "The demons are right. I'll never belong to God. You can see for yourself, I'm sealed with their sign."

I explained to Tony that a wound in his flesh was not an irrevocable pact. It was a clever tactic of the devil. Satan often convinces a victim of possession to sign blasphemous statements or to undergo a physical ritual that claims permanent ownership by evil. Then the person is constantly reminded of this vow by the physical evidence. The devil tries to trick people into believing that, because they have orally uttered blasphemies, they can never be saved—they have committed the unpardonable sin.

I have often encountered this tactic and found it necessary to explain the real nature of the unpardonable sin. This act, blaspheming the Holy Spirit, referred to in Matthew 12:31, Mark 3:29, and Luke 12:10, does not refer to a specific deed. It implies a continual disobedient attitude toward the Holy Spirit by rejecting the person of Christ and His miracles. This deliberate rejection of His grace continues until the capacity to repent and the desire for God are gone.

This is a deliberate act of unbelief that is not committed in ignorance or haste. The Pharisees to whom Jesus directed this condemnation were experts in the law and had persistently harassed Christ with claims that His miracles were the acts of the devil. Furthermore, they made their accusations immediately after watching Him heal the blind and dumb demoniac.

We can conclude from a thorough review of the scriptural instance in question that the unpardonable sin is descriptive of a spiritual state more than the condition of a single reprehensible act. Those whom Christ indicated had committed this sin showed no remorse or repentance toward their sins and displayed no desire to understand the truth of Jesus' words.

Satanic groups try to convince their members that once they have shed innocent blood they can never be forgiven and accepted by God. Such logic is a lie that ignores the substitutionary atonement of Christ who shed His blood to offer us unmerited redemption (Eph. 1:7). There is no crime so heinous or bloodthirsty that it escapes the reach of God's grace.

For those who may feel they have passed beyond the boundaries of God's forgiveness and committed the unpardonable sin, 2 Corinthians 7:10 declares that "godly sorrow produces repentance leading to salvation." "For 'whoever calls on the name of the LORD shall be saved'" (Rom. 10:13) is the promise to those who desire to turn from their wicked ways. The depth of God's love is so unfathomable that He has transformed murderers, adulterers, thieves, and all those who have asked for forgiveness.

ANNULLING THE SEAL OF SATAN

Once Tony realized he was not condemned by the unpardonable sin, we were able to proceed with more resoluteness. I knew that the 666 brand of Satan had to be annulled to remove the legal right of the Christ demon, so I asked the pastor for a glass of water. "Use a paper or plastic cup," I directed, because I had mistakenly handed a glass of water to a demon-possessed person who wanted a drink during a prior exorcism. The spirit promptly manifested, crushed the glass, and tried to injure me with the jagged shards.

When the pastor returned with a cup of water, I held it in my hands for a moment and prayed silently over it. Then I dipped my forefinger in the water and made the sign of the cross over the pink-colored scar of the numbers 666.

I motioned for Tony to take the water. When the cup touched his hands, the Christ demon manifested. His eyes widened and he stared at the cup. "I'm not drinking that!" he yelled. "You can't make me drink that . . . that blood!"

"Oh yes I can!" I demanded and moved in closer.

Tony's pastor looked puzzled. He couldn't grasp the demon's revulsion to a cup of water.

I looked at the pastor and explained. "I prayed that the water in this cup would spiritually represent the blood of Christ, so that when I applied it to Tony's brand it would nullify the meaning of the scars."

The pastor was stunned when he understood that the demon, without my having said a word, saw real blood in that cup. This caused the demon in Tony's body to writhe in torment.

"Grab him," I told the pastor. "Let's hold Tony's head so the Christ spirit can't move it."

He positioned himself to get a better hold of Tony's upper body. I pried open his mouth and forced the contents of the cup down the demon's throat. He screamed and thrashed about violently. Once the contents of the cup had been emptied, the demon went down and Tony returned. He looked suddenly calmer and was docile.

HOW DO DEMONS INTERACT WITH OTHER DEMONS?

During Tony's exorcism, a strange phenomenon occurred. I received a phone call from a young man named Reggie, to whom I had tried to minister deliverance a few weeks earlier. The first time I met Reggie was at a public rally. Reggie came to kill me; he said evil spirits had told him to stab me to death. The attack was thwarted when an alert security guard at the entrance to the auditorium spotted Reggie, sensed he was trouble, and frisked him. The guard removed a six-inch switchblade, hidden in one of the boots he was wearing.

At times Reggie genuinely wanted to be free. On other occasions he appeared unwilling to do what was necessary for his liberty. The timing of his call seemed odd, but I interrupted Tony's exorcism to speak with Reggie; he was in desperate need of help and that's why my office had forwarded the call to me. I took the phone call in a far corner of the room. From the start of the conversation it was obvious that Reggie had not called for help. He was belligerent and verbally abusive. Suddenly one of Reggie's demons manifested.

In my left ear, which was beside the phone receiver, I heard the evil spirit call one of Tony's spirits by name. In my right ear, I heard Tony's demon respond. Yet the voice of Reggie's demon could not be heard in the room. Tony's demon had supernaturally heard Reggie's demon calling out over a distance of more than two thousand miles! It was an uncanny feeling, hearing Reggie's demon call encouragement to Tony's demon, promising that help would be on the way to fight against what I was doing.

Then, an even stranger thing happened. I heard Reggie, in his own voice, say, "I'll take any of Tony's demons that want to come into me!" Before I could react, Tony's body jerked and I heard Reggie scream. He laughed and the phone fell silent.

After this incident, I made repeated attempts to contact Reggie, but he never returned any of my calls. To this day I have no idea what happened to him, but I fear the worst since he was willing to receive some of the demons that had possessed Tony.

Not all unclean spirits interact with one another so cooperatively. There is no honor among thieves, and when demons are on the defensive, it's every unclean spirit for himself. When demons are losing the struggle to stay in someone's body, they will fight among themselves to be the last one to go.

My interrogation of weaker spirits in a demonic system sometimes yields valuable information, which is acquired at a fatal cost to the betraying demon. He may be punished by more powerful demons. More than once I have seen weaker demons scream in torment because a more powerful spirit got even with them.

I have also observed demons fighting with each other. Normally they are bound by a vow of evil to cooperate, like a band of robbers who agree on a scheme for thievery and operate in concert. However, if one member of the team should decide to steal from his fellow thieves and take a bigger cut of the action, the others will turn on him. The same is true with demons. I once dealt with a trio of spirits named Murder, Hate, and Revenge. After a time of prayer and fasting, it became obvious to the most powerful demon,

Murder, that the forces of God were going to prevail. In some way, Murder "killed" the other two demons. He feared they would confess information affecting his ability to stay in the victim.

On occasion I have coaxed one spirit into doing something that betrays another. Often demons are too intelligent to fall into this trap. However, in the heat of spiritual battle demons can become confused and act unwisely. At certain times I have called on God to send an angel of confusion to disrupt the plans of demons and make them more susceptible to our divide-and-conquer tactics.

THE SMELL OF SATAN

At one point during Tony's exorcism, I noticed a foul odor filling the room. I had heard other exorcists say that pungent odors accompany certain demons, but had only experienced it on a couple of occasions. This time the smell was overbearing, like a combination of sewage and rotting meat.

God spoke to my heart and brought the words of 2 Corinthians 2:15–16 to mind: "For we are to God the fragrance of Christ among those who are being saved and among those who are perishing. To the one we are the aroma of death leading to death, and to the other the aroma of life leading to life."

That Scripture led me to say to Tony's pastor, "I want you to bend over with me and gently blow into Tony's face." Both Tony and his pastor looked at me as if I was crazy. "If God has breathed life into us, and if the life of Christ dwells in us, then by faith we can breathe the aroma of Christ onto a demon," I said to them. The pastor and I drew near Tony's

face. Cupping our lips into the shape of an "O," we softly exhaled. At first there was no reaction. Then Tony started squirming and the Christ spirit came forth, cursing ferociously. The demon appeared to be choking. "Get your breath off me! I can't stand it. It's suffocating me!"

"Keep blowing until he goes down all the way again," I instructed the pastor.

What happened when we blew on the Christ spirit? Demons operate with a mystical worldview, and God may use an evil spirit's supernatural interpretation of a phenomenon to exercise His power.

After a few minutes, Tony returned to consciousness. "What was the most repulsive thing you did at your coven's initiation ceremony?" I asked him.

His eyes rolled from side to side as he tried to concentrate. It took a few minute before he could remember. Then his face twisted in a grimace. "The entrails," he said. "I had to eat the entrails."

"What entrails?"

"We sacrificed a pig. I had to pull the entrails out with my bare hands and eat them raw. At the time it didn't make me sick; I guess I was under the demon's influence. Afterward, I threw up for hours and was sick for several days."

The Christ demon came back quickly. "So, now you know." He spat with a sneer. "We got him every way we could. The brand, the human sacrifice, and the curse of the swine."

Now we were getting somewhere. "What's the curse of the swine?" I demanded.

"An ancient curse," the spirit said. "That was our ultimate right to him. I entered when he ate the entrails."

I wondered why that particular deed was so serious, even

more serious than the human sacrifice of an eight-year-old child. Then the Lord showed me. Christ cast demons into a herd of swine as proof of His divinity. As a result, the people of Gadara rejected Christ and asked Him to leave their country (Luke 8:26–39). To satanists, ingesting the entrails of a swine was a way of consuming the essence of an antichrist spirit.

WHERE DOES A DEMON GO WHEN HE IS CAST OUT?

I knew what I had to do for Tony's freedom. I bound the Christ demon and asked Tony to kneel facing me. I was about to do something very strange, but I knew in my heart it was right. I have cast out hundreds of demons, commanding every one of them to go to the pit. The exorcism of Tony is the only time I have not cast a demon into the pit (or the "abyss"). Tony's demons were commanded to go into a pig!

Every time I have cast demons to the pit, they have pleaded not to be sent there. I've confronted demons that screamed, writhed, and begged to avoid the pit. As a practical matter, any place a demon doesn't want to go, is where I want to send them.

Can demons be sent elsewhere? As mentioned earlier, the demons in the demoniac of Gadara were sent into a herd of swine. In another instance Christ commanded unclean spirits to leave and never return again (Mark 9:25). It might be argued that these demons were implicitly sent to the pit, and that they knew their place of doom without a specific command from Christ. It is also clear from Scripture that some demons, which are now bound in the pit, will be loosed again during the tribulation period (Rev. 9:1–3).

Why did I cast Tony's demons into a pig? A better question might be, Why did Jesus permit the demons of the demoniac of Gadara to enter a herd of swine? For one thing, those in Gadara were Jews; raising pork was a violation of the Law. Jesus undoubtedly amplified their disregard for God's holy injunction by allowing their illicit source of income to be destroyed. (I suspect that when the pigs plunged over the cliff and into the lake and were drowned, the demons were automatically consigned to the pit.) Just as Jesus reminded the citizens of Gadara of their sacrilege, I reminded Tony's demons of their grave blasphemy.

BREAKING CURSES OF ALL KINDS

Tony's bondage is an example of spiritual slavery rooted in curses. Ancestral curses are often the most serious and may effect descendants for generations. The story of Ray and Cynthia illustrates how serious such spells may be.

Cynthia and Ray had driven more than two thousand miles to meet with me. Normally, I wouldn't have taken a referral for deliverance counseling, but Cynthia and Ray's pastor was a personal friend and he had pleaded with me to consider helping them. Ray was a superintendent in a large Christian school in the northeastern United States. He was considered one of the best in his profession, but a series of strange events had nearly torn his marriage apart.

When Cynthia and Ray walked into my office, I asked them to be seated on a couch. After we exchanged small talk about their long trip, our conversation centered on Cynthia's struggle with demons.

"I never had a serious spiritual problem of any kind

growing up," Cynthia said. "My parents were Christians, and I always wanted to marry someone in the Lord's work. That's why it's so hard to imagine that I could have a demon."

"How do you know it's a demon?" I inquired.

"That's what we think it is," Ray added. "Why else would she have tried to jump off that bridge?"

"Your pastor told me about that incident. Please repeat the story for me."

"We had driven down that highway a hundred times on our way upstate and often stopped to admire the beauty of the scenery at Windy Ravine. It's a sheer drop-off, plunging over two hundred feet to a raging river below."

"I don't know what came over me!" Cynthia exclaimed, as she broke into sobs. "I love my husband and children. Why would I want to jump?"

She dissolved into uncontrolled weeping as Ray enfolded her in his arms. I offered a couple of tissues from my desk to wipe her tears and waited patiently for her to regain composure. After several moments she calmed down and continued.

"Something in my head kept telling me to climb over the railing and jump to my death. I knew it was wrong, but the urge was overpowering. If Ray hadn't been there to stop me . . ."

Cynthia broke down again. This time Ray took up the story. "I was so stunned I didn't react at first. I thought she was kidding when she put her foot on the railing and started to pull herself over it. I guess it was the look in her eyes . . . that strange look. I'd never seen it before. It was so evil it frightened me, and I knew I had to grab her."

"Describe that look," I said.

"It flashed into her eyes—just for a few seconds—but I felt

I was looking at the devil himself. Someone else seemed to be looking back at me. And that's not all. When I tried to pull her off the railing, she fought back. Afterward, Cynthia told me she didn't remember a thing."

Cynthia broke in again. "I recall Ray stopping the car and suggesting we take a break from the drive to enjoy the scenery for a moment. The fall colors were so beautiful. I remember getting out of the car, and that's it."

There was silence for a moment as they both paused to relieve the tension of their intense account. "What happened after you restrained Cynthia from jumping?" I asked Ray.

"Not much. We were both in a state of shock and got back into the car as quickly as possible and drove off. Neither of us said a thing about what happened the rest of the drive. I suppose I was too confused and Cynthia too embarrassed to discuss it. The subject never came up again until the night that . . ."

Ray paused and looked at Cynthia. He reached out and took her hand as she bit her lip to fight back the emotional pain she was experiencing.

"Have you been to a doctor or some kind of counselor?" I asked.

Both nodded their heads. "Yes, several times," Ray said. "But the night I heard the voice, I was convinced Cynthia's problem is spiritual."

"Is this the male voice your pastor told me about, the one that speaks with a Scottish accent?"

"Yes, and believe me, if you heard it, you'd understand why we're so anxious to see you. It's the scariest thing I've ever encountered, and it comes out of my wife's body. He says his name is the High One, that she belongs to him, and she has to die. The voice goes on and on about now being the time, because Cynthia is the fourteenth."

"The fourteenth what?"

"We don't know."

I saw a faint smirk cross Cynthia's lips as her eyes narrowed slightly. I leaned forward in my chair and fixed my eyes on her. "Who is looking at me? If it isn't Cynthia, I demand in Jesus' name to know who it is."

Ray reassuringly touched Cynthia's arm. For a moment nothing happened, then her muscles tensed and her head tilted back slightly.

"What do you want?" a voice deeper than Cynthia's said with an obvious Scottish accent.

"Are you the High One?"

"I am."

"To whom do you belong?"

"My master, the Evil One."

"Satan?"

"Yes, the true lord of the universe."

"How did you come to possess this body?" I asked.

"I've always been here. I was here before she was born."

"Under threat of torment by the angels of God, tell the truth. When did you enter her"

The High One sighed and gave me an exasperated look. "I told you, before she was born."

I waited for some reaction that would indicate God was executing judgment on the demon for lying, but nothing happened.

"How did you enter before she was born?"

"Through the curse of the elders. She was chosen fourteen

generations ago by the Scottish elders. Now she is mine and she must die."

Four hours later, the High One left. In fact, he begged to go, after Cynthia learned of the curse, renounced it, and broke the spell that had been passed down for fourteen generations.

HOW ARE CURSES BROKEN?

A curse is broken in the same way it is established. If the curse was a verbal commitment, the victim needs to verbally renounce the curse. If ritualistic ceremonialism surrounded the curse, the victim needs to go through certain actions that physically and emotionally express the undoing of the curse. If documents were signed, the victim should write a legal statement, voiding the curse.

Curses are exacting, legal arrangements of the spirit world. Just like human contracts contain fine print and carefully crafted language, satanic curses are often filled with minutiae that require a detailed voiding. In some cases, I've discovered that leaving out one phrase or one word can make all the difference. Satan will exploit the smallest thing to keep the curse in effect.

Stacy was a teenager who sold her soul to the devil to join a witchcraft cult. She wanted to gain popularity that she couldn't obtain in her own social circles. Her curse was known as "drawing down the seventh moon." While leading her in a prayer of renunciation, I referred to the curse as the "drawing down of the moon." After a frustrating time of being unable to make the spirit obey my commands, an intercessor who accompanied me suddenly realized I had left out the word *seventh*. That one word made the difference in breaking Satan's bondage of Stacy's life.

Often those who need to break a curse are so emotionally distraught, it's advisable to lead them in a prayer. Don't rush the prayer. Articulate slowly and carefully so that God can direct you at any moment regarding the exact words to be used. If you write down the curse, be sure the person signs it. If it was a blood curse, whereby the person ingested human blood, you may want to partake of Communion with the victim as a symbol of the person's new allegiance to the blood covenant of Christ.

When breaking generational curses, it is helpful to specifically name any blood relatives involved in the curse. If you don't know the names of the participants, be as specific as your knowledge allows. You might have the possessed person say something like, "I renounce all ancestral links to the curse of [their name], and subject to Christ all known and unknown blood relatives who trafficked in the occult. If any of my ancestors who are pertinent to the voiding of this curse are unknown to me, I ask the Holy Spirit to bring their names before the throne of God to force Satan's submission to the nullifying of this bondage." Curses upon children can be broken by their parents or whomever has been placed in immediate spiritual authority over them. Curses over wives can be broken by husbands. Children themselves can break the curses of their parents by repudiating the sins of fathers and mothers and claiming a new spiritual heirship as members of God's family.

Don't be surprised by the historical extent of curses. The biblical principle expressed in Exodus 34:6–7 indicates that a minimum of four generations may be involved, and the lineage of Satan's claim could extend much further. Make sure that all spirits associated with the curse are thoroughly interrogated to uncover all those affected by the curse.

CASTING OUT TONY'S DEMONS

I opened my Bible to 1 John, chapter 4, and asked Tony to point the forefinger of his right hand to verse 3: "Every spirit that does not confess that Jesus Christ has come in the flesh is not of God. And this is the spirit of the Antichrist . . ."

"Tony, I'm going to lead you in a prayer. Say each word and phrase after me, and mean it with all your heart."

Tony nodded in agreement. I prayed, "I bow in the name of the Lord Jesus Christ. I receive Him as my personal Savior, and nullify the brand of Satan. I receive the seal of the Holy Spirit, the earnest of my inheritance as a child of God. I renounce the curse of the swine and ask Jesus to forgive me for having eaten of the entrails. I repudiate my position as the high priest of the coven of Satan and command that the spirit of antichrist leave me and enter back into the swine from which he came."

This prayer was not spoken as fluently as I have recorded it here. It actually took nearly thirty minutes to say these few words. Every word was resisted by the demon with violent counterattacks and each mention of Jesus was coupled with profane blasphemies, which we had to constantly rebuke. It took the strength of both the pastor and myself to hold Tony under control until each word of the prayer was clearly enunciated. When at last Tony completed his prayer of confession and repentance, he collapsed from sheer exhaustion, weeping for joy. The curse on his life had turned into a blessing of self-acceptance and a recognition of his worth as a creature loved by God.

CHAPTER 8

How Satan Steals, Kills, and Destroys

Not long ago I went to see a local theater production. I sat in the darkened theater, stunned by the theme of the performance on stage. The script, written by a gay Jewish playwright, was filled with clichés and stereotypes about Jewish customs. Actors and actresses portrayed an early twentieth-century Russian Jewish community.

A poor, young Jewish man, smitten with love for a rich man's daughter he could never have, slowly went mad. Finally, in desperation, he uttered twice the unspeakable name of God and, according to Jewish tradition, dropped dead. His spirit then became a *dybbuk,* a demon. Unlike orthodox Jews who believe that demons are fallen angels, the Jews in this play believed in the occult cabalistic idea that demons are souls of the departed. According to this belief, these disembodied spirits have unfinished work on earth, which can only be completed by possessing a human body.

The dybbuk of this play entered the body of his beloved as a way of supernaturally bonding their souls. His presence was discovered by the Jewish Council, which convened to conduct an exorcism on her. In their quest to discover how she had become possessed, the rabbis ferreted out the "legal right" of the dybbuk. To do so they summoned the dybbuk's late father from the dead during an elaborate ceremony. According to the play, the boy's father and the girl's father had long ago pledged their offspring to be married, but the girl's father reneged on the pledge. In the end, the rabbis exorcized the dybbuk, the girl subsequently died, and the two disembodied souls found love in the spirit world.

The play troubled me because it repudiated Jewish biblical theology, and it made a hero out of the dybbuk. I was disgusted by this perversion of Jewish tradition, but it prompted a mental journey backward in time to several years ago when I met a woman named Charlene.

A REAL-LIFE MEETING WITH A DYBBUK

One evening after my message at a Baptist church in the deep South, an attractive thirty-something woman with long blonde hair and a troubled look on her face approached me.

"Mr. Larson, may I have a few moments of your time?" she requested.

I consented and asked the pastor and his wife to accompany me. The four of us sat down in an unoccupied Sunday school classroom.

"You look very disturbed," I commented. "Did something I say tonight upset you?"

"I just got out of the hospital," Charlene said agitatedly. "While I was there, a woman in the bed next to me led me to Christ. When I told her I was being discharged, she suggested that I talk with you if at all possible."

"Why were you in the hospital?"

Charlene stood and reached toward her waist with both hands. She untucked the bottom of her blouse from her slacks and slowly pulled it upward, exposing her midsection. Her entire stomach area looked as if someone had hacked it to pieces with a knife and then sewn it back together with convoluted folds of flesh. I stared at the healing wound, too shocked to respond.

Slowly Charlene lowered her blouse, sat down, and began speaking. "A year ago I came home from a party a little tipsy. I was undressing for bed when it happened."

She paused, and I spoke. "What happened? Did someone attack you?"

Charlene shook her head. "My husband, Stuart, is involved in, shall we say, shady activities. He's Jewish, and years ago he got messed up in a mafialike gang. He fears that someone is trying to kill him, so he keeps a loaded gun in the closet." Charlene pointed her right index finger at her midsection. "For some reason, when I was standing there in the closet, I reached for his gun, placed the barrel against my stomach, and pulled the trigger."

"What were you thinking when you pulled the trigger?"

"I wasn't thinking. In fact, I don't actually remember firing the gun. I only recall seeing the gun and then regaining consciousness just as I pulled the trigger. The next thing I knew, I was awakening in the hospital after surgery." Charlene took several deep breaths. "Can you help me? I need to know why I pulled that trigger and why I still have lingering thoughts of killing myself."

"There are many reasons people are suicidal," I answered. "Some of them are emotional and others are physiological. Have you told all this to a medical doctor and to mental health professionals?"

Charlene wrung her hands nervously and nodded her head affirmatively. "I talked to everybody in the hospital who would listen to me. They put me through all kinds of psychological tests. I spent hours with a shrink. Nobody could find anything in my past that would have made me do this."

"Have you been involved in the occult?"

Charlene shook her head.

"Have any family members practiced witchcraft?"

Again Charlene shook her head no. I concluded that if her problem had a natural explanation, no one, including me, had found it. I had a sense that she was plagued by serious spiritual problems. Conversely, there wasn't any clear indication Charlene had done something that would give a demon the legal right to take over her consciousness and try to take her life.

I decided to pray to see what God might show me. I instructed the others to kneel with me by Charlene's chair. "Lord Jesus Christ," I prayed, "show us who or what is responsible for the attempt to kill Charlene."

As I prayed, Charlene's body shivered and her left shoulder jerked periodically, but no demons manifested. After several minutes of intense prayer, I was almost ready to send Charlene away. Then the Holy Spirit led me to say something that aroused the enemy. "Thank You, Lord Jesus, that You have come to give us abundant life and deliver us from Satan who comes to steal, kill, and destroy."

When I said the word *destroy*, Charlene's body stiffened and her thin wispy voice deepened. "Leave me alone. She's mine!"

"Who is speaking? I demand to know—in the name of Jesus Christ." Charlene's head lifted and her eyes opened. It was the same look that I'd seen in Singapore and countless other times since. "Who are you?" I asked.

"I am Suicide."

"By what sin did you enter this body?"

The spirit shrugged its shoulders. "Nothing in particular. She was easy. She didn't have much backbone to say no to anything. We just waited around until the right moment and the door to her soul opened that night when she got drunk. Now that she's mine, you'll never have her. I'm going to kill her!"

I knew this was going to be a tough fight.

HOW DOES SATAN KILL HIS VICTIMS?

"The thief [the devil] does not come except to steal, and to kill, and to destroy"(John 10:10). To fully understand the meaning of this Scripture and what Suicide intended for Charlene, we must first comprehend why a demon needs to possess a human.

Demons are noncorporeal spirits. They have no physical mechanism to express their will. They need a body to accomplish their heinous designs. The devil tries to control the universe and all of its inhabitants. Just as Christians are ambassadors for Christ (2 Cor. 5:20)—His hands and feet to minister the gospel—Satan seeks human emissaries of evil who will spread his teachings. The most effective way to do this is by controlling the faculties of an individual. But while Satan is using a victim for his purposes, he is also bent on destroying and killing them. That is the *only* way he knows how to operate.

Demons Can Kill a Person's Emotional Expressions

When Jesus referred to Satan killing, He was not only alluding to murderous acts by those under demonic control. Satan also destroys those he invades by "killing" the person's core identity. If successful, demons will establish their character as the center of their victim's emotional expressions. The demons will eventually take over almost all emotive responses and act as a filter for all the person experiences.

When the demonic domination reaches that point, the victim may give up and withdraw so that the will of the demons subjugates nearly all of the original person. People give control to demons because they are hiding from their emotions and life.

For example, if someone rejects the victim, the hurt will be amplified by the demons. What might be a minor brush-off will be made to seem like a major rejection. A mild traffic dispute can turn into murder. Demons intensify every feeling as they act out their duty to torment their victims.

Often demons embolden people who otherwise live reclusive lives. Unclean spirits prey on those who are dysfunctional in relationships and withdrawn in crowds. Like a drunk with too much alcohol, the victims of demons develop a boisterous personality with demonic encouragement. They crave the demon like the drunk craves his liquor, though both ignore the consequences.

Demons Can Kill a Person's Mental Health

Demons not only kill their victims emotionally, they can "kill" them mentally as well. I am frequently asked if those in mental institutions are demon possessed. Some may be, but certainly not all. There are many reasons for insanity, including congenital factors, severe illnesses, hormonal imbalances, disease, and trauma. However, my investigations have personally convinced me that some of those who have been labeled mentally ill are in fact demonized.

This mental demonization and deterioration occur in several ways. First, a mentally sound person may be driven to insanity. The demons kill the normal mental processes and leave behind a shattered mind. Second, a demon that mimics insanity may manifest so frequently that mental health professionals presume this demon is actually the person. Third, a demon may facilitate physical infirmities, which bring about a physiologically diseased state that leads to dementia.

How do you know it isn't a mental problem? I have always approached the possibility of an exorcism cautiously. Most deliverance sessions I've been involved in were the result of a spontaneous demonic eruption that occurred during a conversation or counseling session. The exorcism wasn't planned. Though I have occasionally dealt with demons as the result of a referral or a request for counseling, such instances are rare. When I have agreed to talk with someone who thinks their predicament might be demonic, I carefully follow a regimen of eliminating all possible explanations other than demonic.

The Roman Catholic church has strict procedures before a diocese may authorize an exorcism. These include psychological counseling and the insistence that medical advice is sought. Though I don't have a formal checklist, I use an informal process of elimination to explain away demons. Only after I have exhausted every avenue will I suggest that a deliverance may be necessary.

This rigorous approach helps to eliminate the possibility that the person's problems might be mental. However, even if mental aberrations are present, an exorcism might still be in order. Mental illness may be the result of demonic influence, and mental illness can make one susceptible to demons. This "chicken or the egg" question is resolved by acknowledging that it can be either mental illness or demon possession, or both. There are also mental illnesses that have nothing to do with demons.

Demons Can Deaden the Spirit to Godly Impulses

In addition to attacking the mind, demons may also seek to "kill" the spirit by deadening it to godly impulses. I've ministered to individuals who have had their spiritual acuity so numbed they are almost incapable of desiring the things of God. Such individuals may actually think they are beyond redemption. Only persistent biblical counseling will restore them to a state where they can respond to the Holy Spirit.

In the most extreme example, Satan kills literally by driving the victim of possession to suicide. A demon may so oppress and mentally torment an individual, the person loses perspective on life and despairs to the point of self-destruction.

I was personally acquainted with a pastor who suffered from such oppression. I learned from the pastor's dearest friend that spiritual darkness had haunted him for several years. His mental deterioration was accentuated by demons that tormented him day and night. Unfortunately, this pastor was not part of a denomination that understands and teaches the reality of deliverance, so he didn't know how to pray effectively against these forces.

One Sunday morning before the church worship service, the pastor was acutely despondent. He ate breakfast with his wife and then walked into the bathroom. Moments later his wife heard a loud pop. She thought her husband had dropped something in the bathroom. When she went to see what happened, she found her husband dead on the floor with a gun in his hand.

Did he go to heaven? God alone knows if he was a genuine believer. In the case of Christians who commit suicide, I believe that God judges such people by their spiritual condition when they were last able to think rationally and make spiritual decisions. I also believe that God takes into account the controlling influence of demons that led to the suicide.

Demons also steal from their victims.

How Do Demons Steal from Their Victims?

When Jesus said that Satan steals, you might conclude this refers to individual acts of theft and vandalism. It may, but Satan has other ways of stealing. He steals virginity by sexual temptation, and he steals hope by leaving crushed dreams. Satan purloins the ability to know right from wrong and ravages faith in God and His Word.

The worst damage a demon does is often unseen, as in the

case where a demon robs a person of his self-esteem. I have dealt with demonized people who have been encouraged to commit abhorrent acts while under a spirit's control. A teetotaling Sunday school teacher went on drunken binges. A young single woman engaged in promiscuous sex with anonymous men. A housewife took dangerous doses of street drugs.

I once dealt with a demonized young man who came out of a trance state to discover that his body had been used in perverted sex acts by those in a satanic cult. Even though he wasn't directly responsible for these repugnant deeds, he still felt the shame. This resulted in a severe loss of self-respect.

The devil's destruction is complete when the ability to see the world through God's eyes is gone. Moral conscience evaporates and pleasure is taken in corruption. Satan's theft is fully achieved when relationships with loved ones are stolen and the victim of demon possession is isolated to suffer alone, often to contemplate suicide.

CHARLENE SUMMONS HER HUSBAND

For several hours we battled Charlene's demon of suicide. I used every technique at my disposal to weaken the demon. To some extent I succeeded, but the demon belligerently hung on. Then the Holy Spirit spoke to my heart and said, "Get her husband involved." The spiritual impression was so strong it startled me. I wondered what good it would do to involve her husband since he wasn't a Christian, but I couldn't escape what God was telling me.

I explained to Charlene what I wanted her to do. She immediately objected. "You don't understand," she implored. "My husband is a dangerous man. If he doesn't like what's going on here, he might take it out on you."

I insisted that Charlene call her husband, and she finally agreed. While she phoned from another room, the three of us spent an anxious fifteen minutes waiting to hear his response. When Charlene returned, she appeared distressed.

"I told you he'd be angry at being awakened in the middle of the night to come to a Christian church. Please, let me leave. I'll intercept him on the way over here."

I wasn't certain how much of Charlene's desire to leave was her own choosing and how much was the influence of the demon of suicide. Several times she put on her coat to depart and then sat nervously back down to think it over. She rubbed her stomach, fearfully remembering what the demon of suicide had done to her.

We somehow managed to wait it out, and fifteen minutes later her husband, Stuart, entered the room and everyone froze. His dark black hair, solid six-foot-two-inch frame, and piercing dark eyes accentuated all Charlene's warnings. Anger flared from his face, and he exploded as he stepped through the door.

"What are you doing here! You know I've forbidden you to attend church," he yelled. "Who are these people? And what do they want from us? If it's money, tell them to forget it. And which one is the exorcist?"

Charlene pointed at me. Stuart walked over to me, his arms folded in defiance.

"Maybe my wife needs to see a psychiatrist, but she doesn't need you!" he roared. "Perhaps she's schizophrenic or something like that. If it's a mental problem, we'll deal with it ourselves. I can get her the best help in the state, but this business about demons is insane. What do you think this is, the Dark Ages? Whatever you've got to say to me had better be good, and it had better be quick!"

His eyes bore into me and his big arms were crossed in front of him. I stayed calm and spoke clearly and precisely. I told him we were there to help.

Stuart took several deep breaths to calm himself and sat down, still glaring at me. I began my explanation by reminding Stuart what had happened that awful night when Charlene had pulled the trigger of his gun. I spoke to him about her painful recovery in the hospital, but none of this seemed to affect him. His hatred for me was too intense. As I was about to complete my account of the evening, Charlene interrupted.

"Stu, I'm not sure what he's saying is true or not, but please don't be mad. I can't believe these good people would be lying." She gestured toward the pastor and his wife and gently took Stuart's hand. "Go along with this, just for a little while. If you aren't convinced, then we'll leave."

Stuart softened a little and put his arm around Charlene, pulling her close to him. He seemed to genuinely care about her, and I knew that was my one hope of resolving this impasse.

"All right, you've got ten minutes to prove your case. If you can't, we're out of here."

I didn't have time to pray or deliberate about what to do next. I needed wisdom from the Lord quickly, and it came. I commanded the spirit of suicide to manifest. Almost instantly Charlene's back stiffened, and she drew away from Stuart. I recognized the look of Suicide in her eyes.

"Spirit, I take authority over you in the name of Jesus Christ."

Suicide smirked. He knew I was in a difficult situation and he had the upper hand. The Lord drew my attention to the opposite side of the room. This was a Sunday school room for children and a plastic toy container was against the wall.

"Suicide, I command that you get out of that chair, walk across the room, and sit on that toy box." I pointed toward the plastic container. For a moment Suicide did nothing. "In the name of Jesus I summon mighty angels to stand on either side of you and lift you from that chair and force you to the other side of the room."

Suicide's shoulders seemed to thrust upward as if pressure were being applied at the armpits. Almost weightlessly, he stood and staggered toward the toy box with a look of disgust.

Stuart looked confused, but didn't move.

When Suicide finally sat down, I bound him. "I demand that you allow Charlene to return to consciousness. Charlene, I call you forth."

Suicide wasn't sure what I was trying to do and resisted momentarily. Then gradually Charlene came to her senses. When she was fully aware, she glanced around the room anxiously. She reached down with both hands and felt the sides of the toy box.

"Stu, what am I doing over here?" Charlene asked with genuine perplexity.

Stuart lowered his head. "I don't know, sweetheart. Maybe it's hypnosis or something like that."

It was the reaction I wanted. By having the demon take over Charlene's mind and physically move her to another part of the room, I proved to Stuart that something unusual was happening. The look on his face was one of amazement.

"Charlene, please cooperate with me. I need you to do one more thing," I said softly.

Charlene nodded in agreement.

"Suicide, I command that you come to attention."

Charlene's body jerked, and Suicide manifested.

"Look at her husband and tell him who you are!"

For an intense moment Stuart and Suicide glared at each other. Then Suicide spoke. "I'm a dybbuk."

The blood drained from Stuart's face and his body went limp. All his antagonism disappeared, and tears formed in his eyes. He looked directly at me.

"However you want me to help, I'll cooperate. I speak Yiddish, but my wife doesn't understand the language. She's never been around anyone who speaks it." Stuart paused as I waited to find out what he was talking about. "Dybbuk is Yiddish for *demon*."

Now that Stuart was convinced that Charlene had a demon, I knew what I had to do. Though it went against all my theological presuppositions, I knew in my spirit that Stuart was the one to cast the demon out of his wife!

CAN SOMEONE WHO ISN'T A CHRISTIAN CAST OUT A DEMON?

Christians aren't the only ones who attempt exorcisms. Medicine men, witch doctors, and all sorts of shamans seek to exorcize evil spirits. In primitive cultures, demons are often believed to be the source of illness, spells, and bad luck. Pagans consort with witch doctors who brew potions and perform spells designed to appease or oppose unseen entities. Certain voodoo ceremonies are designed to expel evil spirits through consorting with "good" spirits. In many cases the clients of such occultists seem to experience phenomena similar to that resembling Christian exorcisms. They also achieve a measure of relief from torment. But the demons have tricked them and will usually revisit their victims when they are out of the limelight.

When the Pharisees accused Jesus of casting out demons by Beelzebub, the prince of the devils, Jesus pointed out that a kingdom divided against itself cannot stand (Matt. 12:25). So what is happening when witchcraft is employed to expel an evil spirit? Since Romans 12:21 declares that evil is only overcome with good, we know that evil cannot truly cast out evil. What appears to be a legitimate exorcism may only be the unclean spirit temporarily vacating his human residence to give the impression he is gone. As an alternative, the demon may stay but cease certain actions of torment, giving the impression the pagan exorcism was successful. In either case, no true deliverance has occurred.

What bearing does this knowledge have on understanding Charlene's exorcism by her unbelieving husband? While God is not obligated to honor the prayers of the pagan, no matter how sincere he may be, God *does* respect the hierarchy of spiritual order. Ephesians 5:23 points out that the husband is "the head" of his wife, just as Christ is Lord over the church. Certainly such God-given authority is tempered with responsibility. But setting that charge aside, even a nonbelieving husband has divinely given authority over his wife. In this respect, God holds him accountable for her spiritual condition, but He also grants to him the right of bearing her spiritual covering.

"Repeat after me and mean what you say as a chosen one of Israel," I instructed Stuart, whose hands were shaking.

I slowly spoke the words that sealed Suicide's doom. Stuart never took his eyes off the demon as he repeated after me, "In the name of the God of Israel, He who parted the Red Sea, the cloud by day and the fire by night, I take the authority that is mine as the husband of this woman whom God has given to me. We are one flesh and her body is my body. I command that you leave her body and loose her from your desire for death. Go now to the place God has prepared for you, the pit."

With the same resoluteness that Stuart had opposed me when he entered the room, he confronted the unclean spirit. Suicide grimaced, closed his eyes, and left with a scream.

Charlene crumpled forward on the floor. Stuart rushed to her side, knelt by her, and stroked her face. When she came to they embraced. I sat there amazed that a nonbeliever who had initially denied the reality of demons had successfully helped to complete an exorcism.

When Stuart told the dybbuk to leave his wife, he was not acting on the basis of faith in Christ, and therefore not claiming the sovereign right that would be available to a spirit-filled Christian. He was acting on the basis of conferred authority because of his marital role. Under certain circumstances, a non-Christian may successfully perform an exorcism. In that kind of circumstance, a husband, in conjunction with the authority expressed by a genuine believer, may even evoke the name of Christ as a matter of divine order without personally expressing regenerated faith in the Son of God.

This teaching is not intended to confuse but to encourage those in deliverance to adapt to whatever situation is at hand for the sake of the victim. The night of Charlene's deliverance I might have stubbornly refused her husband's participation. Instead, I welcomed his involvement. This amazing exorcism did not result in Stuart's conversion at that time, but it did achieve Charlene's deliverance. This underscores an important truth: The goal of an exorcism is the freedom of Satan's victim, not conformity to a supposed set of human criteria by which the exorcism must be performed.

God's rain falls on the just and the unjust. He is Lord, and He may choose to heal or deliver a non-Christian. He may also choose to use a non-Christian in the process of another's freedom from disease or demonic bondage. If these cases cause concern, we must let God be God.

CHAPTER 9

The Enigma of Demons and MPD

Randall leaned forward and rubbed his knees. He folded his arms across his chest as if guarding himself from further suffering. Tears formed in his eyes. Though he was a grown man in his mid-thirties, his vulnerability made him seem like a child.

"You don't know how much pain I'm in," he said. "I hurt so badly, I want to leave this room and hide somewhere so I can scream." Randall paused as he strained to form his thoughts. "One thing I'm sure of," he said softly, "I don't have multiple sclerosis, even though I have all the symptoms!"

Randall had barely been able to enter my office. He couldn't have made it without leaning on the arms of his wife and his pastor. He had collapsed on my office couch, and it took minutes for him to catch his breath from the ordeal of navigating from the car to inside the building.

"I had M.S. five years ago, but the Lord healed me," Randall insisted. "I refuse to accept the symptoms I now have, and I'm claiming my healing by faith."

I didn't react to his bold statement. I had seen others claim healing from the Lord in the face of severe symptoms. Some were compelled by their own desire. Others were prodded by healing evangelists who didn't want to admit their failures. When people weren't healed by their prayers, they blamed those who had sought healing, saying they were the ones who lacked faith.

Those who claimed healing as Randall did were often audaciously in denial. In some tragic cases, their refusal to seek competent medical help proved to be physically dangerous. By avoiding proper medical treatment, they allowed their condition to worsen, sometimes beyond remedy.

Somehow Randall seemed different. He was sincere, and I was impressed by his confidence. Randall's wife, a shy lady who listened attentively to every word being said, looked worried and a little nervous. Then Randall told me his M.S. symptoms were the result of demonic influence. He pointed to his pastor, sitting next to him, to back him up.

"Pastor Neil says he confronted evil spirits who spoke through me," Randall explained. "He can describe what he's seen and heard. All I know is that God healed me, and the devil is trying to get me to doubt my healing."

Pastor Neil was a portly man, with a graying beard and balding head. He had sat there nodding in agreement with everything Randall said. When it was his turn, he spoke confidently about the deliverance he had attempted.

"I've been through three exorcisms with Randall," he explained. "Each of them seemed successful at the time, but the demons we cast out were all back in a few days. Worse yet, they brought others with them. Some of the new demons were more powerful than the ones we expelled."

As I listened to his narrative, I marveled that the four of us were together under these circumstances. Pastor Neil had contacted me after a series of radio broadcasts during which I talked about spiritual warfare. His daughter had heard the programs and told her father about me. "Maybe Bob Larson is the one who can help you set Randall free?," she had suggested.

Pastor Neil asked if I would spend some time with Randall. I had hesitated at first, because of my busy schedule. But when I sensed Neil's sincerity, I couldn't refuse. I had arranged this meeting, hoping to offer some advice that would help them make progress in Randall's deliverance.

My first suggestion was aimed at explaining why the same demons kept coming back. "You probably never found the gatekeeper demon. It didn't matter how many demons you cast out, they didn't have to go to the pit because the gatekeeper kept the door open for them to return."

"Gatekeeper?" Pastor Neil asked.

"Yes, the demon who provides continual access to the person's body or soul. Gatekeepers don't have to be powerful demons. In fact they often aren't. They're just clever. They stay hidden so their role goes undetected. But they're most valuable to the entire evil spiritual system in the person. They control the entry for all the others."

Pastor Neil smiled. "I wish we had known that before. We sure could have saved ourselves a lot of sleepless nights." He patted Randall on the shoulder to encourage him. "Can you tell us anything about the demons we encountered?" the pastor asked.

"Possibly. What were their names?"

"I can't remember them all. Murder, Lust, and Violence were three of the most powerful. There were a couple that seemed to be too serious. They called themselves Regulator and Facilitator. The two strangest were Vivinanda and Sridepok."

"The last two sound like East Indian names. They could be Hindu demons. Randall, have you ever been to India?"

Randall had been struggling to listen to the exchange between me and his pastor. He kept rubbing his knee and elbow joints to assuage the pain. "No," he answered, "and I don't know the first thing about Eastern religions."

His wife looked at him and shook her head in agreement. That puzzled me, but I did have a hunch about two of the other names. "Regulator and Facilitator sound like the iden-ities of multiple personality alters, dissociative states of Randall's consciousness."

"Disso what?" Pastor Neil inquired.

"*Dissociative.* A psychological term used to describe a separate mental and emotional identity when a person's mind has fractured into one or more alternate personalities."

"You mean demons?"

"No, Pastor Neil. Demons are much different from alters, as we call them for short. I can understand your problem accepting the idea of different personalities all abiding in one person's mind and body, but it's real."

The look on Pastor Neil's face indicated he wasn't sure about my diagnosis.

"This is not the first case like this I've seen. I first became aware of multiple personalities nearly twenty years ago when

I started ministering deliverance. Back then, no one, including psychologists, were talking about this sort of thing. They certainly didn't have any fancy names for it."

"How did you find out about the alters, as you call them?"

"I was ministering to a man named Phillip who was trying to escape a satanic cult. While I was dealing with demons, an identity surfaced that I could not cast out. It went by a human name—Christopher, a personality that talked and acted like a five-year-old child. That tipped me off."

Randall was now listening so intently, he had stopped rubbing his aching muscles. "How did you know for certain that Christopher wasn't a demon?"

"I wasn't sure, until I tried repeatedly to cast him out. I decided to try a different tactic and talked to Christopher as if he were a person. I discovered that Christopher was the name of a child that Phillip's cult had sacrificed. Phillip told me he was the one originally destined to be sacrificed. To avoid being killed, he tricked Christopher into taking his place. The guilt and remorse so overwhelmed Phillip, he went into dissociative denial. His mind created an identity, an alter named Christopher, to keep him alive. That way, Phillip didn't have to admit to himself what he had done. After all, Christopher was alive in Phillip's mind and lived as a real identity.

"Randall, I suspect there are several layers to your mind and emotions. The person I'm talking to now may not be the real you. For some reason, the core of who you are is hidden. I want to talk to the Randall we all know."

My abruptness shocked everyone in the room. Talking abstractly about multiple personalities was one thing, but trying to talk to one in Randall was different. Yet if Randall had demons, they were listening to what I was saying and were beginning to develop a counteroffensive to my strategy. If the element of surprise was to remain in my control, I needed to confront whatever alters were part of Randall's consciousness.

He immediately straightened and sat back on the couch, looking at me intently. "What are you asking of me?"

Randall's wife and pastor looked equally baffled. If nothing else, Randall's sudden reaction indicated I had touched a sensitive point. I probed further. "Something traumatic happened to you, some time, somewhere. Perhaps when you were so young, you don't remember. Your mind may have experienced selective amnesia and blocked it out. I feel that your thinking and emotions are being regulated carefully; you're under some kind of control by another part of your consciousness."

"You think I'm crazy, is that it?" he argued with a pained sound in his voice.

"I didn't say that. I do think your mind has been fractured by past emotional injury, and the essence of your identity has been submerged. I need the part of you that is hiding to come out."

Randall narrowed his eyes and hugged himself tightly.

Pastor Neil looked at me dubiously. "Randall isn't mentally ill, if that's what you're thinking," he interjected. "He heads up one of the ministries to youth in our church. Not only that, he also has a master's degree in educational psychology. In fact, he's only a few hours away from writing his doctoral thesis."

I thought for a moment. *They still don't understand what I've been trying to explain. I've got to make them understand the difference between demons and dissociated alters or we'll never set Randall free.* (Dissociative identity disorder is the result of severe trauma and has been recognized by the American Psychological Association officially since 1980.)

I leaned forward and patted Randall on the shoulder. His body relaxed a little. "I absolutely don't mean Randall is insane," I said to Pastor Neil. "What I'm talking about is a complex defense mechanism that has probably kept Randall sane and alive. Actually, the fact that his mind developed mentally dissociated identities is proof of his intellectual acumen. Only the brightest people are able to do that. I've known people who have hundreds of multiple personalities and each alter has its own set of personal habits and distinctions. Imagine trying to remember every detail of personal behavior, including the likes of all those separate personalities—all using the same brain power!"

Randall and Pastor Neil seemed relieved. "If there are other personalities inside Randall, how would they differ from a demon?" the pastor asked.

"Think of it in terms of two words: *survival* vs. *destruction,*" I explained. "A demon is there to destroy the person. A multiple personality, an alter, is there to facilitate the person's survival. Often the abuse or emotional trauma was so severe that the person who experienced it would have cracked mentally if they had continued living with the memory of what happened. So part of them encapsulates the memory, along with all its feelings, and splits off. That way the rest of the consciousness can go on without having to remember the hurt or the horror, as in the case of Phillip."

Randall's wife spoke. "Who are these personalities you're talking about? Are they different from the person I know as my husband?"

"Facilitator could be one of them. That doesn't sound like the name of a demon. An alter personality who facilitates would help to smooth over the trauma and minimize the hurt of the memory. Regulator could be some sort of internal mechanism to keep Randall's true feelings under control. That way he wouldn't have to feel any pain from the past."

Pastor Neil stood for a moment and took a couple of steps around the room, as though it helped him to think better. "I understand what you're saying, but how does all of this tie in with demons? I know that I dealt with demons. They were violent and cursed me profanely. That wasn't Randall."

"I agree, it probably wasn't. But the demons could be hiding behind Regulator and Facilitator. They could even be possessing one of these alters."

Pastor Neil shook his head. "Whoa! Wait a minute. Are you saying that a specific alter might have a demon, while the rest of Randall's consciousness does not?"

"Yes, and I'll take it one step further. In the realm of multiple personalities, there are good alters and bad alters. Good alters are the part of the person's consciousness that has acknowledged Christ as Savior. Bad alters, for one reason or another, refuse to make that spiritual surrender. Sometimes bad alters are just spiritually unconvinced identities. At other times these portions of the person are possessed by a demon."

Pastor Neil's frustration was plain as he quickened his striding about the room. "You're telling me that the spirit of a person can be saved, that separate aspects of his consciousness can receive Christ while other aspects reject the Lord? Is that right?"

"Exactly. Our task is to sort through that maze to gain the

assistance of the good alters. Then we can attempt to win the bad alters over to God. At that point, we'll be able to distinguish the identities that are demon possessed and cast them out."

My explanation was interrupted by wailing. Randall, who had been sitting quietly, leaned forward with his head in his hands. His sobbing grew more and more intense until he spoke in a soft, childlike voice.

"I didn't think anyone cared about me. It's been so lonely all these years staying in hiding. But I had to regulate Randall or . . ."

"Or he would have hurt too much?" I inquired.

"Yes," Regulator said between sobs. "I regulate everything about him. When someone says something that hurts him, I don't let him feel the pain. When he's disappointed, I make him believe what happened never really happened. You're not mad at me for doing that, are you?"

"No," I said, "we're not mad at you. In fact, you are very important to Randall's freedom from the demons."

"Are you talking about the dark ones who live in the shadows?"

"Yes. They're not like you. They come from another place and time."

Regulator shook his head. "You can say that again! They appear and disappear. Sometimes there are many of them, and other times just a few." Regulator pulled his knees up under him and hunched his shoulders in fear. "Please don't ask my help to get rid of the dark ones. They frighten me."

"Who can help?" I asked.

Regulator shrugged his shoulders. I glanced at Pastor Neil, who looked totally perplexed at the proceedings. He wasn't alone. I wasn't sure what to do next. More than once I have reached a point in an exorcism where I didn't know what to do. At those times, intercessory prayer was usually the most effective course of action.

I bowed my head and clasped hands with Pastor Neil and Randall's wife. "Lord Jesus, whether You want me to face a demon or alter, bring forth the one who can most help us."

I lifted my head and watched to see what would happen. For a moment nothing. Regulator stared straight ahead, his body still poised in a frightened position. Then he blinked and his face sobered. His body relaxed and he sat erect.

"Let me guess. You're Facilitator. Is that right?"

"I am. But if you think you're getting rid of me—"

"I don't want to get rid of you, and I don't want to get rid of Regulator. I need both of you, but obviously you know some things he doesn't."

"If you're talking about the dark ones, I do. I make certain they don't have any reason to get mad at the rest of us."

"Do you appease them?"

"Let's just say I facilitate everything that goes on internally between those of us who are a part of Randall and those who come from the dark world."

"Do you know how the dark ones got there?"

"Yes, but why should I tell you?"

"Because I come from God. I can get rid of the dark ones if you'll help me."

For the next hour Facilitator and I debated his role in Randall's deliverance. Gradually, I was able to convince him to cooperate. His greatest fear was that any assistance he lent would cause the dark ones to retaliate as they had done before. The Holy Spirit had paved the way for our encounter, and I was eventually able to lead Facilitator to Christ. When I did, his attitude changed to one of willingness.

"Do the names Vivinanda and Sridepok mean anything to you?" I asked.

"They are the most powerful of the dark ones," Facilitator answered. "They were here before I arrived. Regulator knows more about them than I do."

"Do you mind if I talk with Regulator?"

"Not at all. I suspect he's anxious to talk to you."

Facilitator closed his eyes, and Randall's body hunched over again in the fearful pose of Regulator.

"I'm glad you're back, Regulator," I said. A slight smile crossed the face of Regulator, but something didn't seem right. I narrowed my eyes, looked sternly, and decided to test my spiritual hunch. "You are Regulator, but you're not the same Regulator we spoke with. You are a dark one."

The demon let out a cackle. "Very clever of you. There are two of us named Regulator. He's part of this body, and I come from my master."

"Spirit, I bind you in the name of Jesus Christ and command that you tell me what you regulate."

"The same thing as my counterpart—his emotions, his perception of things."

I thought for a moment about what the difference between the alter and the demon could be. The answer came. "You regulate reality. You lie to him. You make him believe that what *is not* is, and that what *is* is not."

The demon looked startled. I knew the Holy Spirit had revealed Regulator's purpose to me, because I couldn't have known it any other way.

"Very, very clever. But it won't do you any good. I can

twist his mind to make him think what I want to make him think. Even now I'm telling him that you are not truly a man of God. By the time you get back to talking to him, he'll be convinced he's got to keep quiet."

"I demand to know who is under you and what other spirits are in your control."

"Pain, that's all. But that's enough."

"Is Pain the one who creates the suffering of the phony multiple sclerosis?"

"My, you are getting this all figured out, aren't you? Of course. Perhaps you'd like to see a sample of what we can do."

Randall's body suddenly jerked and Regulator the demon was gone. I immediately recognized Randall as he doubled over in pain, clutching his right knee. He grimaced for a moment and then said, "I've got to leave. I shouldn't be here. The pain is just too severe."

I remembered the threat of Regulator and dealt with it directly. "Randall, you've been lied to. I know you're not that sure you should be here, and your confidence in me has been shaken. But look at Pastor Neil. You trust him, don't you?"

Randall looked at his pastor and then back at me. I prayed, "I command that angels of God search out and torment the spirit of pain. I bind Pain to Regulator the demon, and command that both of them experience all the torment they've put on Randall. And I increase that torment seven times greater."

My command sent Randall into convulsions. His body twisted and jerked, first in one direction and then the other. He let out a scream. Then he relaxed and Regulator the alter looked at me.

"Do you remember when the dark ones entered?" I asked. Regulator nodded.

"You've got to tell me how it happened. If you don't, the pain Randall has been going through will continue, and he may never be free. You don't want that, do you?"

Regulator shook his head. "I was very little, maybe eight or nine. It was Sunday morning, and a missionary visited our church. He asked if there was anyone there who wanted to give his heart to Jesus. If they did, they were supposed to pray with him, out loud. I whispered to my mother and asked her if I could pray. My mother laughed. She said I was too little and that I didn't understand."

Regulator began weeping. "But I *did* understand. I loved Jesus. I wanted to give my heart to Him. It hurt so bad when my mother laughed, I decided to regulate my emotions so that I would never be laughed at again. Years later, when I finally gave my heart to Jesus, I did it all by myself so no one would know. But it wasn't the same as that Sunday morning. My mother robbed me of something. It has always hurt me very much, deep down inside." Regulator pointed toward his chest.

I had to seize the emotional vulnerability of the moment. Without telling anyone what I was doing, I commanded that Regulator the demon come forward. "Spirit, I demand in Jesus' name that you tell me how what I've just heard allowed you to enter this body."

Regulator locked his eyes on me. "Our little friend, the other Regulator, left out one important detail. That Sunday morning speaker was a missionary from India. Some of my kind had followed the missionary to America. They wanted to keep him from winning souls to Christ when he preached. They seized the opportunity. When little Randall decided to regulate his emotions, it gave them the right of entry. You see, by controlling his feelings that way he was actually resisting the Holy Spirit. He didn't realize that, but they did. It gave them all the legal ground they needed."

"Is that when Vivinanda and Sridepok gained access?"

"Yes, they're the . . ."

"You almost slipped and said too much, didn't you? It doesn't matter anyway, because I know they're the gatekeepers."

Regulator was furious. "Even if you know, it won't do any good. I'm not leaving." Regulator cocked his head back arrogantly. "Don't you think it's interesting how one moment in a child's life could lead to years of suffering from a disease that his body really doesn't have?" The demon threw his head back and laughed viciously.

I had learned all I needed to know. Now I needed to have Randall confess the sin of controlling his emotions in response to the Holy Spirit's conviction and deal with the anger toward his mother. He also needed to see past Regulator's lies that allowed the demon to distort his spiritual perception. These tasks took more than an hour.

As I worked with Randall, I also took time to carefully answer all the questions he and Pastor Neil had about multiple personalities. That evening they both got a crash course in understanding a crucial area of ministry that the body of Christ needs to embrace.

WHAT KINDS OF TRAUMA CAN CREATE MULTIPLE PERSONALITIES?

Multiple personality disorder usually begins in childhood because, unlike adults, children can't run from abuse. The only place they can hide is inside their heads. As the victim grows older, the separate personalities become even more autonomous, and each has its own special way of functioning in the everyday world.

The various alters of a multiple system cope internally like pieces of a pie. Each piece has a limited amount of coping power. When that limit is reached, the switch to a different alter may occur. In this way, the many alters that are part of the system absorb the emotional anguish and physical pain of the trauma.

From time to time one particular alter identity may be "out." When this happens, the host body and core personality of the victim's original identity may lose track of time.

Satanic cult programmers sometimes purposely create alters in victims through the use of trauma—both physical and emotional. Triggers are words or symbols that evoke previously implanted responses. For example, a satanic ritual abuse survivor may be programmed so that every time he sees the color red, a self-mutilating alter will come out and cut the body. Some victims are subjected to advanced programming and are told they will die on a certain date. In satanic cults certain alter personalities are brainwashed to continue attending ceremonies to assure loyalty to the cult.

HOW IS MULTIPLE PERSONALITY DISORDER TREATED?

The treatment of multiple personality disorder requires a comprehensive approach, combining psychological therapy and spiritual intervention. Once the exorcism is over, multiple personalities must be integrated. The one ministering deliverance should be aware that demons that were previously undetected may surface during the integration process. These demons use the dissociative state as a shield and may be forced into the open when the alters are identified and have been integrated (or brought back to union with the core personality).

During the process of treating someone with multiple personalities, a Christian clinician should identify all the alters and help the victim work through traumatic issues for healing and restoration. The final task of the counselor is to allow or encourage the alters in the host's mind to fuse and cancel any remaining demonic ground. Because integration may have to weave its way through inaccurate memories, self-abuse, animal alters, foreign languages, and demonic resistance, complete integration often takes months or years.

Multiple personality disorder disrupts the victim's comprehensive identity and total memory system. Traumatized multiples lose contact with the person God meant them to be. It is important that the Christian community provide a haven for those suffering from dissociative disorder by offering them unconditional love and acceptance. If these people are provided understanding and support, they can once again function normally and offer their considerable talents and mental acuity to the body of Christ. Most important, Christians need to be careful about confusing demon possession with multiple personality disorder.

RANDALL'S DRAMATIC DELIVERANCE

Randall's victory over the demonic forces that had invaded him came when he renounced the sin of his childhood—resisting the Holy Spirit by regulating his emotions. I commanded that the spirit of pain be attached to the demon Regulator, and that he be bound to the unclean spirits Vivinanda and Sridepok. Then I cast out all of them together. While these spirits were leaving, they tried to inflict severe pain on Randall by intensifying the symptoms of multiple sclerosis. This tactic forced me to stop several times and allow Randall to physically recuperate before the exorcism could proceed.

When the demons were finally cast out, all the pain Randall had been suffering disappeared instantly and the symptoms of M.S. vanished. Facilitator and Regulator were no longer needed as distinct identities. They merged into the total consciousness of Randall to become part of his conscious resources, which would assist him in dealing with other life problems. Randall walked from the room under his own power without the slightest limp. Because his dissociative condition was not a complex one, full integration was achieved that night through the healing hand of God. Randall was delivered, but more important, Christ healed and restored him to the wholeness God meant his life to be.

CHAPTER 10

✝ *What I've Seen the Devil Do*

For many people, demons are mythic figures that adorn medieval, religious paintings or make guest appearances in Clive Barker horror movies. Their supernatural deeds are the stuff of Hollywood film editors and computer animation programmers. In modern parlance, the term *demon* represents a metaphor for whatever plagues or torments a person. Any connection of the word with real supernatural entities is dismissed as a primitive explanation for phenomena that ancient man didn't understand.

Yet demons are very real to me, and should be real to all who believe the Bible accounts of evil spirits. Though all Christians can confront demons, only those submitted to Christ's authority should contemplate this awesome responsibility. An exorcism is no place for the merely curious or those seeking spiritual thrills. And an ordained and properly qualified minister should be present if at all possible.

I've included in this book but a fraction of the demonic deeds I've witnessed. Moreover, if I were to chronicle the most dramatic supernatural demonstrations I've experienced, some might be overwhelmed with the information. I want to be sensitive to that fact. I've tried to include accounts that will best illustrate the ways in which Satan operates. The following incidents should serve as a warning to help you understand the dynamics of spiritual warfare. The first story in this chapter shows how bizarre the devil's tactics can be.

SHOCKING DISPLAYS OF THE DEVIL

More than twenty years after Linda Blair played a fictional character whose head rotated 360 degrees as she spat out pea soup in the movie *The Exorcist,* people still ask me if what happened in that movie was accurately portrayed. Some scenes were reasonably authentic, but the more absurd demonic displays were pure Hollywood hype. I've seen more demonic supernaturalism than any living human I've known, but I have yet to witness arms and legs lengthened like rubber bands, heads spinning like tops, and bodies floating in the air. Contrary to myth and occult legend, Satan doesn't display his power in these ways. What I have seen the devil do is remarkable, nonetheless. Christians should be aware of his deception.

I have observed minor acts of levitation. God allowed me to witness a woman, under demonic attack, thrown about a room as if unseen wrestlers were hurling her in a ring. Two pastors assisted me in the exorcism, and it took the combined physical strength of all three of us to keep her from serious injury. As we firmly held on to her, we felt her limbs and torso being yanked in first one direction, then another. Her muscles weren't taut from straining against us. The force we felt from her body was like magnets pulling her in several different directions at once. This battle went on for fifteen minutes until our petition for angelic assistance prevailed. When she finally collapsed, her body was bruised in places where we had not touched her.

This same woman suffered critical internal injuries, which were verified by a physician who examined her. Some of the internal lacerations actually required minor surgery and stitches. In one instance, pieces of wire twisted into shapes that represented death curses were found inside her body and had to be surgically removed. The attending physician had no explanation for the phenomenon of finding solid objects, which somehow had passed through her flesh as if they were immaterial.

Another woman with whom I counseled was assaulted by a sexual demon of incubus. During the exorcism, the spirit said he had come to impregnate her with a devil-child. Along with a pastor, his wife, and the woman's husband, I watched her abdomen supernaturally swell until it expanded to the size of a full-term pregnancy. The complete phenomenon took less than an hour. We countered this demonic impregnation with prayer and commanded that Satan's supernatural offspring be aborted. Gradually, her distended abdomen shrank back to normal size. The spirit was angry because, in his words, we had "killed" his child.

Did the woman's womb truly conceive a half-human, half-demon monster? I doubt it, but what would cause a woman's body to react that way? Every medical doctor knows it takes nine months of hormone stimulation affecting muscle tension and skeletal laxity for the female body to accommodate the baby that is ready to be born. Such physiological conditions occurring in a matter of minutes go way beyond the explanation of medical science.

Some of the most vicious demons I've faced were ones that possessed the body of a young woman named Sharon. As a teenager she joined a black magic sect and witnessed the sacrifice of infants. At the age of twenty-five, she contacted me for help to escape the cult she had once zealously served. The truth of God had slowly dawned on her heart, and she was now becoming fearful that she might be the cult's next sacrifice.

Sharon was afflicted with a demon of suicide. At least a dozen times in the last three years, demons drove her to that desperate act. When I ministered to her, unclean spirits repeatedly tried to choke her and kill her by strangulation. These spirits were so powerful that three or four people were required to physically subdue them.

The most dramatic display of her demons took place late one evening as we neared the end of an exorcism. One bloodthirsty demon knew that Christ was much stronger than he and his legions, and he realized his doom was near. As two men and a woman who assisted me prayed and commanded the demons to leave, we watched in horror as Sharon screamed and writhed. Invisible claws ripped her body until dozens of open wounds seeped with blood. None of us could imagine what was happening. We looked at one another with expressions of utter shock and revulsion.

I was not going to let Satan divert us from what God had called us to do. "You must leave, in the name of Jesus. We will not back down," I said.

The demon held on and inflicted more gashes, even though we prayed and claimed the blood of Christ. Sharon's face, arms, and legs were covered with deep, parallel scratches as if the extended fingers of a hand with claws had been scraped across her skin. We knew similar wounds were all over her body, because we could see blood seeping through the clothing she wore.

As the torment grew more intense, the demon's delaying tactic succeeded: Sharon was in so much pain that we had to stop the exorcism. The woman who was present took Sharon into the bathroom, helped her disrobe, and had her stand in the shower to wash off the blood. Though the demon had gained valuable time to regroup, we were able to resume the exorcism the next day. He was eventually defeated and cast out and did not return. We achieved this final victory because Sharon made a commitment to see herself freed, despite the pain.

THINGS I DIDN'T THINK THE DEVIL COULD DO

Through the years I've learned to not underestimate the supernatural capabilities of the devil. About the time I think I know where the line is drawn on what the devil can and can't do, he performs a feat that defies my presumptions. For instance, does the devil have any right to impersonate a servant of God and thereby deceive a victim of possession? I once thought the answer was "No!" but I learned through practical experience my conclusion was wrong.

I've had people with whom I was ministering deliverance receive phone calls between sessions from a voice they identified as mine. In each case, the voice told them things about their situation that only I would have known. They would converse unknowingly with a demon and would give him important information regarding their deliverance. They had endangered their own spiritual freedom in response to the voice they thought was mine. In some cases, the exorcism was set back days or weeks because of this.

I have even had my physical appearance duplicated by demons. I've received phone calls from people commenting about a recent visit I supposedly made to them. In each case, the victims should have immediately recognized the impersonator because they were told to do something contrary to their spiritual welfare. They obeyed because they were convinced I had actually paid them a visit. The manifestation that they saw seemed credible, not only because of the physical resemblance, but also because the personage again knew things about the victim that only I would have known. Were these human agents of evil who had their appearance altered by a clever makeup artist? Or were these demons taking on physical form and disguising themselves as me? I don't know. But the more important question is "Would God permit a demon or a satanic cult member to do this?"

Some questions are best left unanswered. The more you try to resolve such puzzles, the more paranoid you become. I shrug off such supernatural trickery. I acknowledge what happened, I try to convince the victim of the truth, and then I move forward. It is futile to dwell on how or why the devil does certain things. Such endless speculation does not build faith, and faith is a crucial key to spiritual freedom.

I've also seen the devil mimic the miracles of God through the manipulation of natural laws.

The Case of the Missing Briefcase

I am writing this book on a laptop computer. However, before I entered the information age, I wrote my manuscripts in longhand and then had a secretary type them. Without the current technology of hard drives and backup diskettes to protect documents, my only security was to make a copy of the manuscript. One time I overlooked this practice, and the Lord used that oversight to teach me a valuable spiritual lesson.

I was in the middle of writing a book when I was called to minister deliverance to a woman trying to escape a satanic cult. Her pastor and a woman from her church joined us for the exorcism. The book I was writing had a tight deadline, and I kept the only copy of the manuscript with me so I could work on it when I had a spare moment. At a critical point during the exorcism a demon manifested and said, "Let me see that book you're writing."

The request puzzled me. I assumed it was merely a delaying tactic and responded accordingly. "We're here to cast you out, not look at manuscripts. I command that you obey us in the name of Jesus Christ."

The spirit smirked again and looked toward a far corner of the room where the manuscript, which I kept in a small leather pouch, had been lying on a table. Out of the corner of my eye I glanced in the direction of the manuscript. It wasn't there!

The spirit immediately sensed my distress. "Oh, is your book manuscript missing?" he said mockingly. "If this God you serve is so powerful, why didn't He keep us from taking it?"

I searched in vain for some natural explanation. The exorcism was taking place in the victim's home, and only four people were present. When we had entered the house earlier that day, we had walked straight to the victim's living room where the exorcism took place. No one had left the room since we arrived, and no one had passed through. I wondered if this was a phenomenon I had read about in occult literature—an apport, the disappearance of a physical object and its reappearance at another location. I had previously assumed that apports were really accomplished by trickery, and the devil was taking credit for an illusion.

Yet this couldn't be explained in natural terms. I believe that Satan mimics the miracles of God through the manipulation of natural laws. Satan may have insights into Einstein's theory of relativity—the idea that matter and energy are interchangeable. The phenomenon of dematerialization and rematerialization may be accomplished by transforming the matter into energy, which is then reassembled as matter. (If angels could move the stone from Christ's empty tomb, then fallen angels may have similar power.) Obviously, I don't have the final answer on this issue because I can't comprehend the mysteries of the universe. Furthermore, I don't need to know how the devil can do what he does, since my trust is in God who created all that is to show forth His glory (Ps. 19:1).

I'm embarrassed now to admit that, when the manuscript disappeared, my first reaction was one of anger. The demon's taunt was successful. *If I can't trust God to protect that manuscript, can I trust Him to protect me in other circumstances?* I wondered. And then there was the practical question of the imminent deadline.

I was overwhelmed with discouragement. The demon sensed this and knew he had won a temporary victory. With the emotional state I was in, there was no way to successfully continue the exorcism. I was spiritually weakened.

Perhaps I didn't lay the manuscript on the corner table, I thought. *Maybe there was too much on my mind, and I actually put it somewhere else in the room.*

I yanked cushions from the couch and looked underneath. I moved every object, lifted every sheet of paper, and checked behind every piece of furniture. Even as I conducted my search, I knew it was in vain. A pouch that size holding a thick manuscript couldn't be anywhere else in the room.

Then I began searching elsewhere in the house, from one end to the other. After an hour I returned to the living room and sat dejectedly on the couch. *Why would God permit such a thing at a time when I was in His service?* I wondered.

In the midst of my despair, God's Spirit spoke to my heart. I sensed how ridiculous I had been, frantically running about the house, trying to find the manuscript. I realized the devil was laughing at my predicament and my lack of faith in God. One thought finally passed through my mind: *If God permitted Satan to steal this important manuscript, I have to leave that matter in His hands. God can get that manuscript back for me anytime, anywhere.*

I'm convinced that Satan is often the unwitting accomplice of God's purposes. The devil seeks to bring harm, but what Satan means malevolently God turns to our advantage. As Joseph said regarding the misfortune his brothers brought upon him, "You meant evil against me; but God meant it for good" (Gen. 50:20).

God doesn't toy with us capriciously, but He sometimes lets the devil go further than we think he should to give us an opportunity for spiritual growth. The case of the missing manuscript was my chance to mature in grace and exhibit confidence in God.

I believe God allowed Satan to take that manuscript to see how I would handle it. If I reacted in "the flesh" and tried to get it back by physical means, it wouldn't be returned. If I placed my trust in God, I gave the Lord an opportunity to show that His power is greater than that of the devil. Once I realized this, I stopped looking for the manuscript and prayed.

"Lord, You could have kept the devil from taking that manuscript. If You allowed the devil to take my personal property, I still trust You. Nothing You allow the devil to do to me will shake my confidence."

A peace came over me. I was still concerned about the manuscript, but I was no longer fretting about whether I would get it back. Moments later I felt an urge to walk into one of the bedrooms. I excused myself and headed in that direction. When I stepped inside the room, I saw the pouch lying on top of the bed. I had been in that room minutes earlier and it wasn't there. I walked over to the bed, picked up the pouch, and looked inside. The manuscript was there, not a single page missing.

I returned to continue the exorcism with more faith and power than I had before. Demons that had successfully resisted me before the loss of the manuscript seemed powerless when I commanded them in the name of Jesus. What mattered to me most was not that I had the manuscript, but that my faith in God was restored. I realized, as never before, that my protection from the hand of the enemy is only as good as my trust in God.

This has proved true, even when demons have attempted to kill me.

Attempts on My Life

Once, during an exorcism at a remote mountain location, I had to interrupt the proceedings because of a previously scheduled business phone appointment. It was necessary to drive to a nearby town where there was telephone service. Before I left, a demon warned that he would kill me for what I was doing.

After I finished the call about an hour later, I was driving back to the exorcism site. I rounded a curve and almost ran into a large, black horse standing directly in my path. I slammed on the brakes, veered to the side, and brought the automobile to a screeching halt. The horse stood motionless. Its dark eyes stared directly at me. I glanced down at my trembling hands, and when I looked back it was gone.

Later, when I returned to the scene of the exorcism, the victim of the evil spirits met me at the door. She broke into sobs and thanked God I had returned safely. "The spirits told me you'd never make it back alive," she explained. "They told me they would use an animal to take your life."

I resumed the exorcism in the confidence that God is in control at all times. When the devil is plotting our destruction, the Lord is protecting us from the secret aims of the enemy. As the psalmist declared, ". . . they have hidden their net for me in a pit . . . / Let his net that he has hidden catch himself; / Into that very destruction let him fall" (Ps. 35:7–8).

The Case of Failed Brakes

A year after the black horse incident, I traveled around the world speaking for missionary groups. Just before I left, I was involved in the exorcism of Johnathan, a man who had belonged to a highly secretive black magic cult. I was warned by the demons before they were all cast into the pit that they would retaliate by killing me while I was overseas.

I thought nothing of their threat until I visited South Africa. While there, a Christian businessman loaned me a luxury automobile. I was driving from one church to the next when I approached a busy intersection just outside Johannesburg. I put my foot on the brake pedal and it went all the way to the floor! I saw a car coming into the intersection that would smash into me. Quickly I threw the shift into low gear and pumped the brake pedal again. The car jerked, slowed slightly, and sailed through the red light.

I squinted my eyes and expected a rough jolt. Within seconds my car came to rest by the side of the road, several hundred yards beyond the intersection. I sat up in the car, opened my eyes, and could not believe I had made it through. God's angels must have spared me a disaster. Before I did anything, I paused to thank God in prayer for His hand of safety on my life.

I found a pay phone and called for a tow truck. Then I made a long-distance call to Johnathan, whose demons had threatened to kill me. "Are you all right?" he burst out. "The demons told me that you would be in a serious car accident today. I've been pacing the floor frantically wondering if you were safe."

Later, when my automobile arrived at the repair shop, the mechanic looked it over and shook his head. "This car has a dual braking system," he explained. "It's fail-safe. If one system doesn't activate, there's an electronic backup. In your case, both systems failed simultaneously. I don't see how that could happen!"

Why did God allow the devil to tamper with the brakes and nearly kill me? I favor a different approach to dealing with what happened. Instead of wondering why God let it happen, I prefer to praise God, knowing that Satan's attempt to harm me was unsuccessful. I may have had a close call, but I wasn't killed or injured. My involvement in spiritual warfare made me vulnerable to the devil's attack, but Satan wasn't able to do what he wanted. God stayed the hand of evil from accomplishing all that the enemy intended.

God has blessed me with discernment concerning spiritistic phenomena, and I never treat the devil's displays as if they are a sideshow. I encounter these demonstrations with the armor of God (Eph. 6:10–17); in fact, I often go through the physical motions of actually putting on the defensive and offensive weapons Paul described in Ephesians.

As I enter into struggles of demonic warfare I always remember that Satan is an impostor. He's a loser, not a winner. He is desperately trying to duplicate God's miraculous power. Like the smoke and mirrors of a Hollywood set, the devil advances his purposes through deception, trickery, and intimidation. I have a healthy respect for what the devil can do, but I also know that, compared to God, Satan dwells with maggots and worms and has been "brought down" to the "lowest depths of the Pit" (Isa. 14:11–12, 15). I do admonish demons, but I am cautious about rebuking the devil myself. Instead, I follow the example of the archangel Michael, who declared to Satan, "The Lord rebuke you!" (Jude 9).

One final story will show you how God can fight these spiritual battles for us by guiding our thoughts and actions.

THE STORY OF THE WHITE HORSE

Janie was dedicated to the devil before she was born. Her parents and grandparents performed a prenatal ceremony, giving Satan all claims to Janie's life. Her earliest memories were of spirits manifesting to her. These demons, who appeared as imaginary playmates, seemed to mean no harm.

That changed when she became a young adult. At twenty years of age her psychic curiosities led to her involvement in a secret occult group that practiced a form of esoteric black magic. Janie was the mistress of the cult's leader and became pregnant by him. When the child was born, the cult forced her to kill the baby as a sacrifice to Satan. This led to multiple personality fragmentation and demonic possession.

I first met Janie when she journeyed far from her home-town to attend a rally where I spoke. She had previously written to me, seeking help for her dissociative disorder. I agreed to see her briefly, but minutes into the conversation, demons manifested. Soon I was involved in a full-blown exorcism. Unfortunately, the deliverance session had to be terminated when I encountered a demon who spoke only in a foreign language. I was unable to deal directly with the spirit without an interpreter. We met again more than a year later for an additional exorcism, which also ended without total victory.

Nearly two years after our initial meeting, Janie contacted me a third time, desperate for help. The demons controlling her had revealed that when her parents dedicated her to the devil, they specified a certain year and a time Janie would be sacrificed. MPD alters inside her were programmed to commit suicide on that date. That day was three weeks away!

"They will take my life," she cried during our phone

conversation. "There are parts of me that I can't control. I'm going to die if you don't help me."

I agreed to meet with her at the earliest possible date. Two weeks before her death date, a pastor friend and I met with Janie for a final six-hour exorcism. After casting out several minor spirits, we learned that the controlling demon was a spirit who referred to himself as "Double-D," a reference to his functions of death and destruction.

"You'll never get past me," Double-D bragged. "I'm going to kill her, and I'll kill you too."

"You'll have to get past him first," I said confidently, gesturing over my right shoulder with my thumb.

The demon's eyes left my gaze for a moment and he looked over my shoulder. Terror filled his eyes.

"He's big, isn't he?" I said, believing that I was guarded from the threats of Double-D by a large angel.

"Yes, he is, but I'll still get you somehow," Double-D insisted.

For two hours I did everything possible to weaken Double-D, but got nowhere. I paused in the exorcism and silently prayed for wisdom from God. The demon had been in Janie's life since the prenatal ritual, and the legal ground of his curse was one of the most tenacious I've ever faced.

As I prayed, two things came to mind. First, I remembered that Janie loved horses. Each time we met, she showed me pictures of the many horses she had raised and ridden. The sweater she was wearing that night had a horse knitted on the front. I knew in my spirit that this had a connection with her deliverance, but I couldn't see the correlation.

Then a second image entered my mind. Earlier that afternoon my wife had taken a walk with our daughter in her stroller, and they had stopped in the gift shop in our hotel lobby. My child reached out from the stroller and grasped a small white toy horse. She clutched it so earnestly, my wife wasn't able to leave the store until she purchased it. The rest of that day, my daughter wouldn't let go of that horse. The last thing I remembered seeing as I said good-bye to my wife and child and left to meet Janie was my baby daughter embracing that toy white horse.

God's purpose became clear. I began speaking under the leading of the Holy Spirit, even before all the thoughts of my mind had developed. Without saying a word to Janie or my pastor friend, I reached for my Bible and turned to Revelation, the sixth chapter. I stared into the face of Double-D and read the words of verse 8: "So I looked, and behold, a pale norse. And the name of him who sat on it was Death."

I fixed my eyes on Double-D. "You are the rider of that pale horse."

The spirit responded in shock and defiance. Finally he said, "Now that you know who I am, what are you going to do about it?"

Remember your daughter's white horse, the Holy Spirit spoke to my heart.

The words of Revelation 19:11 came to me: "Now I saw heaven opened, and behold, a white horse. And He who sat on him was called Faithful and True, and in righteousness He judges and makes war."

I quickly flipped through the pages of my Bible to confirm what God had shown me. I commanded Double-D to submerge. The demon knew I was up to something and didn't go down easily, but my persistent commands caused him to cease manifesting.

As Janie came back to herself, I looked at her intently. "I'm going to ask you to do something very unusual. Please cooperate. Your freedom depends on it."

"I'll do anything. I don't want to die."

"Please close your eyes. Relax for a moment and tell me what you see."

My spirit leaped for joy when Janie said, "I see a beautiful pasture with a white horse at the far end of the field."

"What is the horse doing?"

"He's coming my way. He's getting closer and closer."

"Have you ever ridden bareback?"

"Many times."

"When that white horse reaches you, I want you to grab his mane and leap on top of him, and ride away."

A few minutes later tears seeped through Janie's lashes and trickled down her cheeks. A glorious smile filled her face.

"Have you climbed aboard the white horse?"

"Yes! I'm riding away across the pasture."

"Are you alone on that horse?"

Janie smiled broadly and wept for joy. "No! He is riding with me."

"As you ride away, Janie, claim your freedom from the curse of death, in the name of Jesus."

I paused for a moment and then spoke forcefully. "Double-D, your curse over Janie's life has come to an end. I bind both parts of you, death and destruction together, and command that you function as one. Come to attention and face the judgment of God."

Janie's body jolted and Double-D manifested with both arms flailing and legs kicking. It took all the strength from me and my pastor friend to restrain the demon's violence.

"You know who's riding with Janie on that horse, don't you? I command that you confess His name!"

"He who is Faithful and True," Double-D screamed.

I handed my open Bible to my pastor friend and pointed to Revelation 19:11.

"Double-D, Christ Himself has come to set Janie free. He rides away with her now, and as she exercises her faith in Him, your curse over her life is ended. Go now to the pit, in the name of the Lord Jesus Christ."

Double-D looked at me calmly. He spoke almost in a whisper with a resolute tone. "I'll make you a deal. Back off now, and you can have what you want. Go ahead, ask anything of me. You know my master has the right to offer you everything in this world. You can have what you wish, if you'll stop now."

Without hesitating, I spoke back. "In Jesus Christ I have all that I need. In Him is fullness of joy and life everlasting. You can't give that, and what you have to give I don't need and I don't want. I rebuke your offer and command that you leave Janie now."

Double-D struggled again, lashing out with his feet and fists. He screamed at the top of his lungs, "No, don't let Him strike me with His sword."

My eyes glanced down to my open Bible: "'Now out of His mouth goes a sharp sword . . .'" (Rev. 19:15).

Double-D made one last violent lunge, let forth a piercing scream, and left.

God's love and power is always victorious!

Janie slowly regained consciousness. As her eyes opened, a glow spread across her face. "I'm free. I really feel it for the first time in my life." She wiped away her tears with a handful of tissues I gave her. "I must ask you one question. How did you know I've always wanted a white horse? From my earliest memories as a child, I always dreamed that I would someday ride away on a white horse to escape all the evil in my life."

To those who might argue that it seems unfair for an unborn child like Janie to be dedicated to the devil, don't miss the lesson of this supernatural story. As a small child, God put in Janie's heart the hope that someday her deliverer would come. The white horse that she saw through childlike eyes was God's way of foretelling His final triumph.

A POSTSCRIPT

These supernatural stories are extreme examples of how far Satan will go to destroy the lives of those he targets. Most who minister deliverance will never encounter anything near this. By uncovering what the devil can do, we expose his deception. We also reveal the extraordinary efforts of Satan to hold on to his ground in the lives of victims. If the devil cares that much about the souls of those whom he would destroy, how much more must a loving God care about those for whom He died on the cross.

Before you read on, keep this chapter in perspective. It's not what the devil did that I want you to remember. Never forget, my message is this: No matter how tenaciously evil tries to hang on to its territory, God always wins in the lives of those who cry out to Him for mercy. The stunning exhibitions of Satan's pitiful power can be overcome by the might of God as demonstrated by the resurrection of Christ!

PART THREE

Delivering Those with Demons

CHAPTER 11

✝ *The Exorcist*

Pastor Cooper, a godly pastor of a small church, was an extremely effective man of God in an exorcism, even though his denomination taught that anyone who did exorcisms was an unscriptural fanatic. If you asked ministers in Pastor Cooper's denomination to describe an exorcism, they would paint a picture of a mentally ill person surrounded by maniacs screaming at the top of their lungs in an atmosphere of total chaos. This group believes that exorcisms are unnecessary in our current dispensation, and that casting out demons was used only as a sign of His divinity. According to their opinion, present-day deliverance is something practiced by wild-eyed fanatics who suffer from an overdose of enthusiasm, unsupported by proper biblical exegesis.

Pastor Cooper didn't harbor those prejudices. When a woman in his church manifested demons, he refused to sign a pledge saying he would cease being involved in ministering deliverance to her. As a result, he was expelled from his denomination, and he was completely ostracized by pastors who had once been his theological comrades.

Pastor Cooper introduced me to the woman whom he had diagnosed as demonic. As a child she had been severely abused. One time her parents locked her in a closet for three days without food or water to punish her. During that time a spirit appeared to her and offered to take over the role of her parents. "She wanted a new mommy and daddy," the chief demon sneered, when he manifested during the exorcism. "We were only too happy to oblige her."

This rejection of parental authority gave legal ground for a demon to enter. Freedom for this woman finally came after an all-night session of battling demons. Pastor Cooper, who was in his mid-sixties, fought the demons vigorously. His willingness to risk his ministerial credentials for the sake of one parishioner greatly impressed me. His quiet confidence in the calling of God on his life gave him the courage to do what no one in his denomination had done before. If Pastor Cooper overcame his theological inhibitions to engage in exorcism, any Christian can do the same if he or she is called by God.

Every Christian can and should be ready to cast out demons. However, most don't because Satan has convinced them it's not their calling or it's too dangerous or it's theologically inappropriate. The truth Satan wants hidden is that the necessary authority to demolish demonic strongholds is given to us by the Holy Spirit when we are born again in Christ. Believers in Christ have been crucified, raised, and seated in the heavenlies with Christ far above all demonic powers (Eph. 1:18—2:6). Like a royal title, our authority to deal with the devil is a birthright of our status as joint heirs with Jesus Christ. "I give you the authority to trample on serpents and scorpions," Christ told His disciples in Luke 10:19.

Just as a policeman packs a pistol to prove he has the power to enforce the authority of his badge, Christians have the Holy Spirit as a source of supernatural strength to enforce the authority God has given us in Christ. "You shall receive power when the Holy Spirit has come upon you," Acts 1:8 tells us. But authority and power are pointless without faith.

Where does that faith come from? We're given the source in Romans 10:17: "So then faith comes by hearing, and hearing by the *word* of God" (emphasis added). To the exorcist, faith is a radical confidence that God's Word means exactly what it says and that God is faithful.

I have seen this biblical truth at work on many occasions. I remember one time a demon placed his victim in a trance and caused her body temperature to drop dramatically, nearly to the point of death. Her lips turned blue and her flesh was cold and clammy. By faith I took God's Word literally. The Holy Spirit brought to my mind Psalm 119, verse 105: "Your Word is a lamp to my feet / And a light to my path." I spread open the pages of my Bible and held it above the victim's body.

"In the name of Jesus, I command that God's Word shine as a heat lamp on the body of this one whom Satan has attacked. May the radiant warmth of this lamp bring life back to this body," I prayed aloud.

The demon causing this phenomenon manifested and violently tried to rip the Bible from my hands. Those assisting me restrained the interference until God's Word had proved effective, and health and strength were restored to the woman's body.

Christians who are thinking about a ministry of exorcism always ask me about the physical and spiritual dangers. Let's look at those now.

DOES THE EXORCIST FACE PHYSICAL DANGER?

When I first got involved in exorcisms, I presumed that God would unequivocally protect me from physical injury. My naïveté was shattered the day I faced Karen's demon. Karen was a frail, somewhat shy woman whose abuse of prescription drugs had led to severe forms of demonic bondage. The more she relied on drugs to bolster her behavior, the more Satan became entrenched in her emotions.

Our encounter took place in a church meeting room, where only steel folding chairs were available to sit on. I placed my chair directly in front of Karen, as close as possible, so I could stare into the demons' eyes. I assumed that my authority in Christ would allow me to instantly command their obedience.

Yet one of the demons threatened to strike me for rebuking him.

"Sit in that chair. Don't move, you are bound by the Holy Spirit," I commanded.

Before I knew what was happening, the demon tilted his chair back slightly, drew Karen's knees toward her chest, and quickly thrust her feet forward. Karen's feet landed on my chest and knocked me backward off the chair. The steel chair collapsed on the floor as I landed bruised and embarrassed. With as little show of surprise as I could muster, I picked up the folding chair and sat back down. This time, however, I placed the chair a full three feet away from Karen. I didn't trust God's Word any less, but my prudence had been given a new dose of reality.

On another occasion, while battling a physically violent demon, the Lord brought to my mind Ecclesiastes 4:12, which says, "A threefold cord is not quickly broken." By faith, I went through the motions of binding the demon's arms and legs to the chair with an invisible cord. After that the demon tried in vain to move his arms and legs as if he were struggling against actual bonds on his hands and feet. The demon was literally restrained because I acted on the basis of God's Word.

I have seen this technique work on many other occasions, but there have been times when the procedure failed miserably. In certain instances I called on mighty angels to restrain demons. That, too, has sometimes proved effective, but not always. I've learned that certain kinds of demons can be restrained by verbal authority, and others by literally applying Scripture, as with the instance of the threefold cord. No technique is universally applicable. The strength and ability of each demon must be determined at the time of the exorcism as the Holy Spirit gives insight and wisdom.

During one recent exorcism, the victim of possession was so violent, I could only control her by making her lie flat on her back on the floor. Prayer warriors who had joined with me assisted in the restraint. Two people held each of her legs steady, and two other people held each of her arms. A fifth person sat near the top of her body to immobilize her head so the demon couldn't bang it against the floor and injure her. A sixth person applied pressure to her shoulders to keep the demon from trying to raise her back off the floor.

A deliverance session is emotionally and physically exhausting. If the exorcist has to be involved in the physical restraint of the victim, his focus is distracted from the mental and spiritual struggle taking place. Unless I inadvertently encounter a case of possession alone, I always make sure that others are present to help.

In spite of all my efforts to be cautious, I have come away from exorcisms with bite marks, bruises, and deep scratches. If the victim is a woman, and if I expect the ordeal to be physically violent, I may ask her to trim her fingernails before we start. Demons will try to claw your eyes out or inflict injury with long fingernails, and I was severely scratched several times before I learned to take this precaution.

The most humiliating form of physical assault is being spat upon. More than once I've been drenched in the course of an exorcism. Take for example the case of a woman named Susan, who was a lesbian. When her demon manifested, he expressed his hatred toward my manhood by spitting. It happened so many times I finally got a towel, hung it around my neck, and continuously wiped the spittle from my face.

When Susan periodically came out of the trance and saw the humiliation I had gone through, sitting there with a wet towel wrapped around my neck, she was deeply touched. The fact that I was willing to suffer personal embarrassment and revulsion on her behalf was a key to her freedom.

When conducting deliverance, avoid presumptions about what the devil can and cannot do physically to the exorcist. My confidence in God is not based on whether a particular demon may injure me in the course of spiritual battle. Even the best trained soldiers sometimes get wounded in combat. When I am fighting for the freedom of a soul, I expect no less. I always keep in mind the ultimate defeat of the demon. Praise God the question isn't "*If* the person will be delivered," but rather "*When* will that happen?"

DOES THE EXORCIST FACE SPIRITUAL DANGER?

Spiritual competence, not spiritual perfection, is the qualification for being an exorcist. Authority over Satan is based on the righteousness of Christ, not on our spiritual achievements. More than once I've been involved in an exorcism when I didn't feel adequate for the task. Perhaps it was a period of discouragement when my faith was shaken. At other times I entertained feelings of anger or thoughts of carnality.

If the exorcist has unresolved issues between him and the Lord, this will hinder the deliverance: bitterness toward a family member, anger about a disappointment in life, or despair over some unanswered prayer. We are, after all, human vessels subject to all the foibles and failures of our fallen condition. Being involved in the deliverance of a demon-possessed soul reminds us that our only hope for salvation is in the grace of God—not by any good deeds we perform.

If I know in advance I'm going to be involved in a deliverance, I may spend extra time in prayer and engage in a specified period of fasting. If I encounter the exorcism unannounced, I mentally survey my spiritual state. If I feel inadequate at that time, I stop and pray for forgiveness and ask the Holy Spirit to freshly fill my life and cleanse me from any impurities that would hinder the power of God's Spirit from working through me.

Is fasting necessary? Many reference Matthew 17:21, in which Jesus pointed out that certain kinds of demons could only be expelled through prayer and fasting. Some believe this passage means that fasting has some implicit merit. That may be, but the main purpose of fasting is to draw one's attention away from the satisfaction of the flesh and to focus instead on the realm of the spirit. I have fasted several days prior to an exorcism and still found myself with sufficient energy and spiritual focus.

Sometimes in the middle of an exorcism I have stopped the procedure to spend time in prayer and fasting. This renewal can block out distractions and spiritually reenergize the mind and emotions. There is no rule to be followed regarding fasting. It is a spiritual discipline to be utilized whenever God impresses it upon the exorcist that the demons require such diligence.

The most important spiritual preparation for deliverance is a constant state of willingness to be used by God. Such a surrendered attitude of availability protects the exorcist from spiritual dangers. Anyone who presumptuously engages in an exorcism should be warned that trying to cast out a demon is dangerous if you are outside the will of God. Exorcism demands a spiritual stamina that is forged by years of trials and testing that have solidified faith in God and His Word.

Could a demon enter the exorcist if he or she were spiritually unprepared? No! Such fiction was suggested by the movie *The Exorcist*. The priest, unable to achieve deliverance any other way, invited the demon into his own body, which led to his death. The scriptwriter suggested this as a noble act of sacrifice. No biblically grounded exorcist would ever consider such a foolhardy course of action. To the contrary, the true spiritual exorcist has confidence that God can and will set the victim free. This is accomplished through the authority of Jesus Christ, not by the exorcist exchanging his soul for the victim's.

I do want to caution those involved in deliverance to be careful about the individuals who assist you. Consider whether these persons are acting in faith or whether they have offered their services out of curiosity; such selfish motives might make them vulnerable to demonic attack. I always carefully question those who wish to assist, particularly if I am away from home, where I do not know all the people involved.

I warn potential assistants that demons will exploit any lack of unity in the bond of believers engaged in the deliverance. I add, "You could also be subject to mental and emotional harassment if you have unconfessed, serious sin in your lives." Then I ask, "Can you assure me that you are walking closely with the Lord?"

Sometimes potential intercessors have excused themselves because they felt spiritually unprepared. I don't consider this a sign of weakness. I would prefer that an individual admit his shortcomings rather than get involved in something that could prove injurious to both himself and others.

PRACTICAL CONSIDERATIONS FOR AN EXORCISM

Some of the questions I am asked most frequently pertain to practical considerations regarding one's involvement in an exorcism. For example, What does one wear to an exorcism?

If I know in advance, I like to wear comfortable, casual,

loose-fitting clothing. The possibility of a physical struggle and a lengthy session warrants that those involved be as much at ease as possible. When I haven't had the privilege of such preparation, I've been involved in exorcisms while wearing a business suit and dress shirt. Several times I've had this clothing torn or stained during a violent exorcism.

What should you take to an exorcism?

Items That Should Be Present at an Exorcism

Take your own Bible so you can readily find passages of Scripture. I also recommend having more than one translation available. Many contemporary churches use the New International Version, but I often find that the language of the King James or New King James is better suited to a literal translation of Scripture.

A good concordance is also important. The ones in most Bibles are brief so it is best to have a separate concordance, such as *Strong's Exhaustive Concordance*. The Holy Spirit may bring to your mind certain Scriptures to use in battling the demons, and your ability to locate that Scripture and apply it precisely might depend on a complete, unabridged concordance.

If your ordeal is long and arduous, the victim often experiences extreme thirst. Sometimes light, healthy snacks are helpful if you are breaking your fast. Remember, when David was fighting and his troops were hungry, he went into the house of God and ate the bread off the altar (1 Sam. 21:6, Matt. 12:3–4). This act would normally have been unlawful, but as Jesus pointed out, the human necessity of the moment was more important than abiding by strict legalistic edicts.

I have also found it helpful to have a portable cassette

player with tapes of praise and worship music. While taking a break from the ordeal to rest or rethink what is happening, the tapes are a means of torment to the demons and a further invitation for God's presence to be with you.

Make sure that toilet facilities are readily accessible, and never let the victim go into the rest room alone, once the demons have been aroused. If the exorcist is male and the victim is female, it's important to have another woman present who can assist in this regard. If the victim is offended by such seeming immodesty, at least make sure that someone stands next to the bathroom door and that the door is left slightly ajar. I've had demons manifest once the victim was in the bathroom and lock the door. By holding the victim in a trance state, the demons kept the person in the bathroom for hours, and thus stopped the exorcism.

I have also encountered circumstances when a demon tried to provoke suicide while the person was in the bathroom. Medicine cabinets often contain scissors, razor blades, or other sharp objects. Demons will stop at nothing to impede the exorcism, and those ministering deliverance must constantly be on guard for any delaying tactic.

Maintaining the Proper Atmosphere

Above all, there must be an atmosphere of faith and authority in Christ. Let me share an illustration that underscores this. I once engaged in an exorcism with a woman who channeled evil spirits as a spiritualistic medium. Soon after we started, I was distracted by odd noises, rapping and racket, from outside the room where we were meeting. Doors slammed and I could hear creaks and groans in the building structure.

The more I tried to go forward, the more I was distracted by the presence of demons all around us. Then the Lord showed me what was happening. I was reacting fearfully to the pandemonium encircling us, and this was inhibiting my ability to face the forces of darkness with the authority of Christ. I stopped the exorcism, withdrew for a few moments, and prayed alone that God would restore to me "power, love, and a sound mind," according to 2 Timothy 1:7.

By the time I finished praying, the sounds had ceased, and I was able to resume the exorcism successfully. It was then that God also showed me that what the demons were doing to distract me had not ceased. What had stopped was my ability to hear what was going on. The distracting sounds were supernatural, and my spirit was, supernaturally, "hearing" them. I had listened to them through an attitude of fear rather than faith. When I put my spirit in proper alignment with God and began to operate by faith, my spirit could no longer hear them.

In addition, those involved in an exorcism need to be led by the Holy Spirit so that they are absolutely certain their participation is ordained by God. Having determined that, and having approached the deliverance with proper prayer and preparation, each of those seeking to free a soul from Satan will abide in an atmosphere of faith. Satan has already been defeated by Jesus Christ, and we are merely the executioners of God's judgment.

Probably the toughest question to answer is, "When do you know the time is right to start the exorcism?" I agonize over that decision every time I'm involved. Waiting too long gives the enemy an opportunity to build up strength and develop strategy. Prematurely initiating the exorcism can be emotionally traumatic for the victim. Staring into the victim's eyes and commanding demons to come forth can be devastating if it doesn't occur in God's perfect timing. If the exorcism has been planned in advance and the person needing deliverance is aware of what is going to happen, there's no need to delay once everyone is ready to proceed.

Impromptu exorcisms are a different matter. If I am unsure about the presence of demons, or if the victim is edgy about the procedure, I take all the time that is necessary to wait on the Lord for Satan's hand to be tipped. This may be done by spending time in prayer or singing hymns. Such activities create an atmosphere of spiritual intensity that antagonizes demons and causes them to voluntarily come forward without the exorcist having to confront them. In a situation like this, I respond to the reactions of the demons and deal with whatever spirit manifests as a result of what is happening.

As long as the one ministering deliverance proceeds cautiously, and all participants are willingly submitted to Christ, there is no need to be concerned that the timing will be inappropriate. It is crucial that the exorcist begin calmly, quietly, and methodically. Those who rush into an exorcism and make it a noisy, boisterous affair run the risk that spiritual discernment will be lost in the confusion. Other intercessors around him may pray, but the exorcist should quietly pray to himself, keeping his eyes open and focused on the victim.

CHAPTER 12

Preparing for an Exorcism

The screams and commotion from the rear of the sanctuary instantly caught my attention. I had just completed addressing a large audience in a midwestern church, and I was answering questions. The outburst sounded like a violent fight of some sort, so I rushed to the back of the church. A half dozen people were standing around a young woman who thrashed about on the floor. They screamed Bible verses and waved their arms in the air as if shadowboxing an unseen foe.

Several of the would-be exorcists knelt by the woman and tried to physically restrain her arms and legs. "You can't have her. We rebuke you in Jesus' name," one yelled. Another added, "Come out of her and go to the pit!"

The girl kicked and fought back all the more aggressively. "She belongs to me. I'm not leaving!" a hideous voice screamed, salting his protests with curses.

The moment those gathered around the girl spotted me, they motioned for me to join them. "Thank God you're here," one person said. "Now we can get rid of the demons possessing this girl. You'll know what to do."

I acknowledged their pleas for assistance, but something didn't seem right. As politely as possible, I tried to calm down the amateur exorcists. Several cooperated, but the others had no interest in abating their assault on the forces of darkness. They ignored me and screamed all the louder. Quickly I took spiritual authority and insisted that everyone be quiet to bring order to the situation.

The victim regained her composure. She wrapped her arms around her legs, pulled her knees to her chest, and huddled in a corner. She seemed frightened and equally put off by my intervention. I asked everyone to step aside so I could talk to her alone. They reluctantly agreed, and I helped the woman to her feet. We walked to a nearby church pew where she sat down and stared straight ahead, sulking.

The exorcists retired to a far corner of the sanctuary and continued praying. Their boisterous mumblings of threats against the devil were undoubtedly sincere, but I wondered if their prayers were less a petition to God and more a show of defiance toward me.

"What's your name?" I asked.

"Cheryl," the young woman answered. "Are you going to get rid of the demons in me?"

I leaned against the pew next to her. "That depends on whether or not you want me to, and whether or not you have demons."

Cheryl sat up straight with a defiant look on her face.

"What do you mean *if* I have demons? Didn't you see what was happening a few minutes ago?"

"Yes, but that doesn't prove you have demons."

"Look, you don't know how humiliating it is to be thrown on the floor and roll around like that. If you really cared, you'd help me instead of questioning me."

Her belligerence indicated I had touched a sensitive nerve. "How do you know you have demons?" I asked.

"Are you calling me a liar? Do you think this is some kind of act?"

"I didn't say that. I just want to know where you got the idea you have demons."

"She told me, the lady in the blue dress," Cheryl said, pointing to a woman in the far corner of the room. "She prophesied over me and said God told her that's why I cut myself."

Cheryl stretched out her right arm and with her left hand pulled back the sleeve of her sweater. Her wrist was criss-crossed with deep gashes, now healed over by scar tissue.

I gently touched her wrist. "How many times have you done this?"

Cheryl was silent for a moment. "Six or seven times, I don't know for sure," she said, shrugging her shoulders.

"What do your parents think about this?"

Cheryl glared at me intensely. "Parents? What parents? I don't know who my dad is, and my mother dumped me in a foster home when I was thirteen."

I was convinced that Cheryl's antics had nothing to do with demon possession. To be certain, I talked with her for another half hour, interspersing my conversation with words and phrases that would normally antagonize a demon. All the while, I did not take my eyes off hers. Not once did I see that look. I knew my test wasn't foolproof, but it was a strong indication that I was on the right track.

"When you were rolling around on the floor a while ago, how did you feel when one of the ladies rebuked the spirit of witchcraft?"

"I wanted it to be gone."

I leaned forward and touched Cheryl's shoulder. "Cheryl, if you were demon possessed, you wouldn't have heard what that woman said. At the time you were supposedly in a trance with a demon manifesting. You couldn't have known what was going on. But you did, didn't you? You heard every word those ladies said, and you remember everything that happened, don't you?"

Cheryl lowered her eyes slightly, and tears streamed down her cheeks. "You're right. I put on an act. I don't know why I did it."

Cheryl wept and buried her face in her hands. I reached into my pocket and handed her my handkerchief and sat down on the church pew next to her.

"It's okay, I understand. You were just going along with what that woman said, hoping that it would help. Then, the more you went along with it, the more you became the center of attention.

"When people thought you were just a mixed-up girl with emotional problems, nobody took the time to help you. But when they thought you had a demon, they spent hours with you. Cheryl, if I had been through what you've been through, I might have done the same."

Cheryl looked up with a slight smile on her face. She knew that I understood, and she was relieved to finally know the truth.

THE DANGER OF DIAGNOSING DEMONS

Get ready for a shocking statement. Cheryl isn't an exception. I spend more time convincing people they *don't* have demons than I spend time casting demons out of people who do have them.

Some people, like Cheryl, are susceptible to the idea that they have a demon because it quickly simplifies all their problems. It lets them avoid the tough task of dealing with an array of emotional problems. And for the over zealous exorcist, a demonic diagnosis is a quick way to help someone. I've met many people who have been through pseudo-deliverances and have been emotionally scarred as a result. The trauma of having people surround you, shouting insistent rebukes, can be mentally disturbing. Worse yet, if the victim of presumed possession goes along with the ruse long enough, he or she also accepts the false diagnosis, and everyone involved becomes party to perpetuating the lie. Meanwhile, the person's real problem goes unresolved.

After the exorcist determines that the person is truly demon possessed, the next question is naturally: When is the person ready for the exorcism?

When Is the Person Ready for an Exorcism?

The presence of a demon doesn't necessitate the immediate act of exorcism. Some Christians erroneously assume that if a demon is manifesting and challenging the saints of God, retaliatory measures must be taken right away. In fact, not everyone who has a demon is ready to be exorcised. Three factors affect this decision: the volitional willingness of the victim, the spiritual preparedness of the exorcist, and the weakened condition of the demon.

Not everyone with a demon wants to get rid of him. Codependence with a demon (which we will discuss later in this chapter) or a desire for the temporary benefits spirit possession can offer will prevent some people from seeking help. Even those who want to be free are not always volitionally cooperative. The victim may have been threatened with harm to them or to family members.

Trust is also a big issue. Does the victim really trust the exorcist? Does the victim really trust God? *Wanting* to be free and *willing* to be free are different. The will of the victim is the spiritual battleground on which the war of exorcism is fought. The slightest reluctance can mean defeat.

For example, issues that need to be resolved may arise in the midst of an exorcism. This is where biblical ministry must blend with a sound psychological understanding of how trauma affects the soul. During a recent deliverance session with a woman, I discovered that an act of incest had been committed by her father. The woman lived in denial about the incident. She wanted to be free from the demons, but found it difficult to admit that the father she loved so deeply had violated her as a young child. Her initial unwillingness to admit what happened gave the demons legal grounds for remaining.

The willingness of the victims can also be affected by their feelings toward God. Some have been tormented by cults in which satanists, posing as religious figures, brutalized them. They were raped with crucifixes, forced to drink blood in mock communions, or watched as cult members in clerical garb committed unspeakable atrocities. Logic tells them not to equate these horrible deeds with the exorcism, but on a deep emotional level the link remains. Victims may will to be free, but a full volitional surrender depends on a 100 percent mental and emotional acknowledgment of that desire.

When to Start an Exorcism

The strength of the demon may be the most important factor determining when to start an exorcism. I've known people whom I refused to help until they matured in the Lord to the point Satan didn't want them any longer. Though every demon insists he won't leave, some are so tormented by the spiritual life of the victim, they will accept any excuse to go. In fact, I've had demons say to me, "We really don't want to be here. One of the higher-ups made us stay, but we're glad to go. We're sick of all this Jesus stuff."

The role of prayer must be impressed upon everyone involved. Those who assist with intercession by praying apart from the action of the exorcism are just as important as those who face the demons and rebuke them face-to-face. If I can plan the exorcism in advance, I always try to have prayer warriors in another part of the building; they are the ones who worry unclean spirits the most by making them truly sick of all the "Jesus stuff."

The power of the demon can also be affected by things in the victim's life that haven't been dealt with. Unbroken curses, fetish objects still in their possession, and minor occult practices they continue to indulge in will be toeholds the demon exploits. A material object of obsessive greed or an unconfessed anger toward God over some past discouragement will be enough to allow the demon to continue resistance.

Once while conducting an exorcism in my home, I was

hampered by a Balinese wooden carving I purchased as a souvenir while traveling in the Far East. While dealing with the primary demon, I noticed he constantly fixed his gaze on this object, which was sitting on a shelf at the far side of the room.

"What's so interesting about that carving?" I demanded to know in the name of Jesus.

"I'm drawing strength from it," the demon confessed.

Without hesitation, I halted the exorcism and built a fire in my fireplace. When the flames were sufficient, I threw in the carving. It was a hot summer day and the intensity of the fire was almost unbearable, but it seemed appropriate for the occasion. As I watched the carving consumed by the fire, the Holy Spirit reminded me of the words of Deuteronomy 7:26: "Nor shall you bring an abomination into your house, lest you be doomed to destruction like it. You shall utterly detest it and utterly abhor it, for it is an accursed thing."

When the last remnants of the carving crumbled into embers, I returned to the exorcism and readily cast out the demon. This experience makes me wonder how many other victims of demonic attack fail to receive their complete deliverance because they or the one ministering to them has harbored some object or action that is displeasing to the Lord.

Some African and Asian masks depict actual demons. Certain sculptures are intended to convey the presence of a pagan deity. Amulets, fetishes, and souvenir pictures that tourists routinely purchase may transmit curses and hexes. Kachina dolls, dream catchers, yin and yang signs, and other occult paraphernalia don't belong in Christian homes. Though such symbols and objects may be considered spiritually benign, any association with them could hinder one's ability to effectively wage spiritual warfare. These comments aren't intended to be judgmental. My concern is to encourage Christians to look around and rid themselves of anything that could assist the forces of evil.

CAN A PERSON BE DELIVERED BY LONG-DISTANCE?

Several years ago, while hosting my nationally syndicated radio talk show, I received a phone call from someone who purported to be thirteen years of age. She sounded desperate and frightened. Her name was Rebecca and she said she was destined to be a human sacrifice on Halloween. Rebecca called several times over the next couple of days. During one conversation a deeper female voice spoke, claiming to be Rebecca's mother, Catherine. I confronted Catherine about Rebecca's claims, and other voices started speaking to me, some of them in foreign languages. It took days to sort out all the confusion because my only contact was through the phone calls.

I eventually learned that Catherine and Rebecca were actually multiple personalities of yet another identity. And I detected that several of the voices, including one that spoke with a German dialect, were demons. For the first time in my ministry, and for the first time in the history of broadcasting, a live exorcism was nationally broadcast. I rebuked the demons, bound them in the name of the Lord Jesus Christ, and cast out several of them. When the radio broadcast was over, I continued the exorcism via telephone for several days. Yet I was unable to cast out all the demons in absentia. Thankfully, the victim of these unclean spirits received direct personal counseling and deliverance from a compassionate ministry. Many of her alter personalities were integrated and the demons were confronted and cast out.

After this strange incident, I encountered other cases of demon possession during my broadcasts. Although I would have preferred dealing with these people face-to-face in a private setting, I had no choice. In most instances I didn't know the true identity of the person, and I had no phone number to contact the person off the air. Consequently, there was no way the person could be followed up by a local counselor. Some of the situations were life-threatening and a delay to pursue more appropriate circumstances could have been fatal. The limited success of these long-distance exorcisms was the best I could do, given the extenuating circumstances.

Some people suffering demonic attacks, who could not travel to meet me in person, pleaded for me to minister deliverance by telephone. I have done so when possible, and I am sure those prayers thwarted Satan's plans. However, I know of only one instance when I prayed for someone over the telephone and they were completely freed.

Unfortunately, long-distance exorcisms can give Satan the upper hand. The unclean spirit can manifest and use the victim's body to make him or her hang up the phone. In addition, without seeing the victim, the one ministering deliverance has no idea when a demon is manifesting unless the spirit speaks. Several times in this book I have noted how important it is for the exorcist to maintain eye contact with the victim. Often, the spirit's presence is first manifested through the eyes. Also, certain spirits evoke specific kinds of body language when they are present, and the exorcist cannot spot these signs over the phone.

The most important reason to avoid long-distance exorcisms is the potential harm to the host. It is common for demons to injure their victims, especially when the spirit knows he is losing the battle. I have dealt with demons who flailed their victim's head about, trying to bang it against a wall or on the floor to cause a concussion. Some demons twisted arms and fingers out of their sockets, or clawed at eyes. On many occasions, I've had to restrain demons from trying to kill their victims. Some have reached for knives, scissors, or other sharp objects to stab the host. One demon tried to hurl the victim's body through a plate glass window. Others have tried to make the victim drink poison or jump out of upper-story windows.

STRANGE DEPENDENCY ON DEMONS

The case of a woman named Amanda, who lived in a small community in the northwestern United States, illustrates demonic dependency. Amanda was the church organist, a timid, plain-looking woman. Her print cotton dress, decorated in an outdated pattern, reached to her knees. Her straight hair was pulled back into a bun, and she wore rimmed eyeglasses. She spoke with a squeaky voice, and her eyes averted people's glances. Amanda's schoolmarmish appearance belied the horrible truth about her private existence.

I met her at the conclusion of a speaking engagement when she asked if she could confide in me about a problem. We talked for quite a while before she mustered her courage to tell me what was on her heart.

"I'm an alcoholic, and no one knows it," she said tearfully.

"I hide my drinking at home. I teach piano lessons to children and never have to leave the house, except to go to the store to buy groceries . . . and liquor. My piano students don't detect the problem, and I always sober up and get rid of the evidence before my husband gets home. He doesn't suspect a thing."

The longer we conversed, the more it became obvious to me that Amanda's drinking was compulsively controlled by a demon. I know that identifying a demon of alcoholism, or a demon of any other disease or disorder, is suspect to many, so let me discuss that now.

Demons and Diseases

I have dealt with demons of all sorts of illnesses and addictions, from cerebral palsy to schizophrenia and from heroin addiction to compulsive masturbation. This is not to say that such maladies or urges are always the result of a demon. I am not suggesting that anyone afflicted by a physical or emotional weakness is controlled by evil spirits.

My counseling experiences have taught me that demons both exploit physical abnormalities and encourage aberrational behavior. For example, a demon may have known a person was genetically predisposed to alcohol addiction. The demon tempted the person to over indulge in alcohol and then capitalized on the resulting dependency by displaying its functions through the disease's symptoms. Eventually, the distinction between the disease and the demon becomes blurred until both manifest simultaneously.

In the case of a physical infirmity, the demon may mimic the ailments of a disease by afflicting psycho motor and neurosensory functions, or exacerbate the disorder's symptoms until the demon's influence is barely distinguishable from the primary illness. For example, a demon of anorexia would intensify his victim's abhorrent self-image to the point that food avoidance would be virtually a simultaneous demonic and physiological manifestation.

The discerning counselor who encounters a demon manipulating the realm of mental, emotional, or physiological disorders must carefully discern between the source of natural and supernatural factors afflicting the victim. Sometimes, medical attention may be necessary before an exorcism is attempted. The victim of anorexia may first need intravenous feeding to restore metabolic balance, which will lessen the demon's ability to use his victim's weakness. The alcoholic plagued by a demon may first need to dry out and recover physical strength so the demon no longer can enmesh his function with the features of his victim's disease.

Every disease isn't a demon, but any disease may be exploited or imitated by a demon. Proper medical advice, spiritual insight, and conscientious care for the victim's condition will direct the exorcist to the right path for restoring total spiritual and physical well-being. In Amanda's case, I immediately told her that I suspected demonic intervention.

Amanda's Possession

Amanda did not reject the idea. In fact, she replied, "I know it. I even know when he came in—one weekend a year ago during a drunken binge when my husband was out of town on business. What's difficult about all this, is that part of me doesn't want the demon to go."

I led Amanda to a chair and had her sit opposite me while I tried to contact the demon. Calling the spirit of alcoholism forth was easy. He arrogantly presented himself. "What do you want with me?"

"Do you make her drink?"

"Oh no," Alcohol said, "she does that quite well herself. When she's under my influence, I give her boldness she wouldn't have otherwise"

"What do you mean by that?"

"Look at her. She's pathetic. No personality, no gumption. What can you expect, the strict way her parents raised her, like a nun? She never developed socially. Now, *I* do that for her. That's why she wants me."

I commanded the demon to recede and called back Amanda. "Is it true that you actually like the demon of alcohol?"

"I don't like him in the sense that he's a friend. I like what he does for me. I married my husband because he was the first boy I ever dated. Part of me wants to break out of that mold and live a little dangerously. Of course, I can't do that, being the church organist. But when I drink and the demon takes over, I become someone I've always wanted to be— daring, outspoken. The few people outside the church that I see during the day when I'm drunk tell me they like me. If being that person means having a demon, so be it."

Amanda put her face in her hands and wept. After a few minutes she regained her composure and looked at me decisively. "Thank you for your time, Mr. Larson. I'm sorry to have troubled you. I just can't give up my drinking, and I know that if I don't do that, you can't make Alcohol go."

She stood and walked away. It's one of the few times I've faced a case of demon possession and couldn't proceed to spiritual victory. In every instance where I've found a demon could not be cast out, it was because the demon gave the victim some benefit he or she wasn't willing to live without.

CAN A PERSON BE DELIVERED WITHOUT KNOWING IT?

Are there cases of people who had demons and were spontaneously set free through some spiritual process other than an exorcism? If someone needs to be freed from demons, and God loves that person enough to want him or her freed, why couldn't the Lord Himself do the deliverance without the assistance of an exorcist? This is a difficult question to answer since any such occurrence would likely have happened without anyone knowing it. Theoretically, there is nothing biblical to prohibit such a phenomenon, but it is probably very rare. God usually acts through exorcists, just as He acts through Christians to declare His gospel.

God could send an angel to preach to everyone who needs salvation. Or He could manifest Himself supernaturally to convict each soul. Instead, the Scriptures declare that we are "ambassadors for Christ" (2 Cor. 5:20), sent in God's place as human vessels to witness to His saving grace. This is a great mystery of the gospel, that God has condescended to convey the plan of salvation by human instruments.

He works the same way to bring deliverance. "I was in prison and you came to Me," Jesus said in Matthew 25:36. Certainly, those bound by demons are in the worst kind of prison. The exorcist who brings them the truth of God's freedom also ministers unto the Lord. Loving them and speaking words of deliverance to such captives is becoming the hands and feet of Jesus, to walk where He would walk and deliver those whom He would set free.

A FINAL WORD

An exorcism isn't an action, rather it's a process by which the victim of the devil is led from demonic captivity to spiritual wholeness. That bondage may be the illusion of possession (as in Cheryl's case), or it may be an unhealthy demonic dependency. Whatever the circumstances, no force of darkness can forever resist the united effort of a victim who wills to be free and an exorcist who humbly ministers as unto the Lord.

CHAPTER 13

Anatomy of an Exorcism

Your pulse surges with such intensity, the veins on your neck bulge. Your palms grow sweaty, and your tongue sticks to the roof of your mouth. You're like a sprinter in the blocks, awaiting the words, "Ready, set, go." In this case you fire the starting shot by issuing the demand: "Demon, I command that you manifest in the name of Jesus."

Any exorcism is a trial in spiritual fortitude, but doing it the first time requires an immeasurable step of faith. You've read the suggestions in this book. You've prayed and consulted your pastor and other spiritual leaders. Now, it's down to you and the demon. What if you work up this courage to confront the forces of darkness and nothing happens?

Relax. Everyone who encounters an exorcism for the first time approaches it with anxiety and apprehension. Since you will have prayed about the situation, God will honor your forthrightness, even if your diagnosis is in error. So long as you approach the possible victim of possession with gentleness and understanding—and you have their full cooperation—the rest is up to God.

Sometimes, nothing happens. But that doesn't mean your suspicions were incorrect. Often my first attempt to provoke a demon in a person who is genuinely possessed elicits no reaction. The demon may be away at that moment, he may be in hiding, or he might be powerful enough to resist my initial demands made upon him, especially if I am the least bit hesitant.

How does it feel to be involved in an exorcism? For those who have experienced many of them, it's like a brain surgeon performing one of many thousands of operations; he moves confidently because he understands the precise procedures. Yet the first time he cut open a cranium, his hands were probably shaking so badly, he feared he would injure the patient. With experience and repetition, he mastered the austere technique. For me, after all these years, every exorcism is still a humbling, awesome experience. It confronts my human weaknesses and the limitations of my natural wisdom.

Though every deliverance session has its own unique characteristics, there is a general flow to the procedure. Like an exploratory medical diagnosis, the initial stages require more questions than answers. The experience might be explained as looking at the jumbled pieces of a jigsaw puzzle that has been dropped on a table. Yet unlike the puzzle, the disparate pieces of an exorcism are invisible, so figuring out how they are interwoven requires a high level of imagination. The unseen must be fathomed by faith.

God *does* give insight as to what to pursue and how far to

go. The more we know of how evil men and demons work, the better we are prepared to unravel the problems and apply the truth of the Word of God for healing. It is the truth of Christ and His authority that set prisoners free.

When an exorcism is going well, you feel transported outside yourself into a dimension of the supernatural seldom experienced in any other part of Christian living. As you seek wisdom from the Lord, God places thoughts into your mind that seem absurd at the time. Don't resist them. Probe, experiment, step out in faith, and remember that each step toward victory leads you deeper into the realm of the non-rational. Be willing to be used by the Holy Spirit in extraordinary ways, without abandoning faithfulness to biblical guidelines.

When an exorcism isn't going well, you will feel intense spiritual stress as if your soul, to some degree, is in a vise grip, with pressure being slowly applied. The exorcist is under constant supernatural attack. The real battleground is the soul of the victim, but your heart and mind are also under assault. I have experienced times when my thinking processes were so tense it was difficult to go from one thought to another. I had to stop the exorcism and step away from the situation to renew my emotional and spiritual energy.

An exorcism can also be the most spiritually exhilarating experience on earth. The Bible comes alive as you see that the forces of evil must obey God's Word. As James said, demons really do believe the truth of Scripture, and they tremble when confronted with God and His Word (James 2:19).

I never leave an exorcism discouraged. I may be disappointed if I was not able to accomplish all that I felt God desired on the pathway to the victim's freedom. However, the obvious presence of the Holy Spirit, which envelopes an exorcism, leaves my mind centered on God and His glory, not Satan and his lies.

Others who have been present when I conducted exorcisms tell me that their lasting impression is one of renewed interest in God's Word and greater dedication to faithful Christian living. An exorcism is a microcosmic display of all the scriptural truths we take by faith but are allowed to glimpse in action.

It is amazing what we are privileged to hear, watch, and witness on behalf of the Lord, for His glory. Hearing demons scream in torment as they are cast into the pit underscores the reality of eternal punishment and the promise of heaven's home. Observing the hatred that demons have for the blood of Christ gives new meaning to the Atonement.

An exorcism is similar to a masterfully played chess game. We must expect abrupt and unexpected changes in the flow of events as a normal part of the process. Planning ahead is vital. The frustration of the exorcist is the aim of every demon. Staying calm and focused disrupts Satan's strategy.

The basic focus of every exorcism is forcing the demon to acknowledge the authority of Christ and demanding that the unclean spirit acknowledge the authority of the exorcist and the victim. No matter what else happens, these two fundamentals should always occur. Demons must constantly be reminded that God is in control and that the exorcist is confident of eventual victory.

As you have seen from some of the stories in this book, there will be times when the one ministering deliverance gets distracted or discouraged. These are only temporary setbacks in God's purpose of deliverance and healing for the victim. Accept the fact that you are a frail human vessel, totally dependent on the Holy Spirit. Admit the superior knowledge of demons when compared to human understanding. But remember that, in spite of your natural incapacities, God's love for the victim will prevail. Don't ever let these truths leave your mind.

In the hundreds of exorcisms I've been involved in, certain moments stand out. One such instance was the time I methodically eliminated the defenses of a certain demon. Step by step I cornered the adversary until he could no longer resist. Before his final doom was pronounced, the demon looked at me quizzically. "Who taught you the rules?" he asked curiously.

"What do you mean by that?" I asked.

"The spiritual rules that determine what we can and can't do. Someone from our side must have taught you. I've never met anyone who knows the rules as well as you do."

The observation of this evil spirit was more profound than you might realize. While no human being has *all* the answers about how to successfully conduct an exorcism, basic guidelines determine the success or failure of any deliverance.

TEN RULES OF AN EXORCISM

I've spent a lifetime garnering information about exorcisms, and I'm thankful to share it with you.

Certain aspects of these rules may have been touched on earlier in this book. If they are reiterated here it is because I want to emphasize their importance and provide additional details not previously underscored. Here are the ten rules to follow as an anatomy of an exorcism.

1. Bind Lesser Demons to Their Leader

Dealing with demons in aggregate shortens the exorcism process. Demonic systems often have more than one demon assigned to a particular function, so they can be grouped together according to their kind. For example, spirits of lust might work in concert with spirits of pornography and perversion. Another coalition may involve a demon of murder with one of suicide. These could be coupled with a blocking spirit used to induce trance states. Groups of spirits may split into several parts, so groups should be bound together as a whole. Some combinations operate like a wrestling tag team, one taking on the exorcist while the other one rests. All groups of spirits have a hierarchical structure, and those of lower rank function in union with all those above them.

Some spirits will cleverly separate from their function. For example, a spirit of perversion, which causes homosexuality, may be cast out under the name Perversion; however, Perversion may have split off his function so the victim is still plagued by feelings of homosexuality. A spirit of hate, which has been driving his victim to thoughts of murder, might leave under the directive of the exorcist, who casts out the spirit of hate. But by splitting off the function of murder, the victim will continue to suffer as if the spirit of hate had not been expelled.

Complicated? Absolutely. It is difficult to figure out all the details of demon tactics and the procedures of exorcism. The faithful exorcist should not despair. God may give the ability to discern who the spirits are and what they are doing at just the right time. As deceptive as the actions of demons are, God is faithful in leading the spiritually sensitive exorcist to determine how to deal with the many variables. The exorcist is not alone. The Lord Himself promises to bring about Satan's defeat. He is standing by your side every moment of spiritual warfare.

2. Work Through the System

One of the initial goals in an exorcism is to find the pecking order of demons. The arrangement of evil spirits in a demonic system is like that of a military command. Each unclean spirit has jurisdictional responsibility over some part of the emotional and spiritual life of the victim. This network is arranged in a hierarchy of ascending spiritual power. To dismantle this infrastructure, I have found it advisable in some cases to begin at the bottom and work up. That's why I sometimes ask God to reveal which demon is the weakest. Then I attack that particular demon since the other spirits above tend to draw strength from those below them.

There have been times when I started out at the top and worked downward. Those rare occasions were in cases where the demonic system was small. If a dozen or more demons possess a person, the exorcist may want to identify the weakest spirit and start there. More than likely this will be a demon that hasn't been in the victim as long as the others, or it is a demon with a function that isn't totally enmeshed in the emotions of the victim. However, the exorcist may spend a lot of time at lower ranks of demons and be kept from the controlling leader. One must be flexible.

Sometimes demons toward the bottom will reveal secrets about those above them, making the casting out of the ascendant spirits much easier. Spirits at the top are generally more intelligent and powerful demons and less likely to let critical information slip out. Remember, there are biblical ranks of demons that are designated in descending order as thrones, dominions, principalities, powers, and spirits.

Someone should be designated to keep a log of the information received while interrogating the demons. As the internal structure of the victim's demonic system is revealed, list the spirits according to their ranking, cite their right and occasion of entry, and note their legal ground for remaining. Think of the person taking notes as filling the role of a court reporter, ready to read back prior testimony as the jury deliberates its decision.

A lot happens quickly during an exorcism, and sometimes the key to casting out a certain spirit will be related to what another demon, perhaps much lower in rank, revealed in earlier questioning. The written log will help you refer back to crucial facts that otherwise might have been forgotten.

As the end of the exorcism nears, it's wise to consult the log one final time. Go through the list of spirits dealt with and interrogate any left to be certain that no part of the entities listed has missed complete detection. The demons will be forced to give you this information because they must submit to the name of Jesus and His authority.

3. Ask God for Angelic Assistance

I've already given several illustrations of intervention by angelic hosts. As Elisha declared to his servant, ". . . those who are with us are more than those who are with them" (2 Kings 6:16).

There is biblical precedent for the idea of angels providing help. Daniel, chapter 10, addresses the issue of angelic assistance. Verse 13 indicates that God's messenger was hindered by a demon that delayed the angel from completing his mission for twenty-one days. It is apparent from this reference that demons struggle against angels. Even though angels are more powerful in their uncorrupted state, they still must fight to overcome the resistance of unclean spirits.

How are angels invoked? I am careful to avoid any attitude that would suggest that angels can be called upon whimsically. Asking God for angels shouldn't be treated casually, as if you were calling the family pet. I usually say something like: "I call on the Lord to dispatch mighty angels for assistance in dealing with the demons before me."

Designate the angels' function. Angels may be asked to guard from external demons seeking to interfere. Angels may be requested to bind or restrain the demon to lessen the demon's physical resistance. Angels can also be used to intimidate demons as a way of weakening their resolve. Many times I have halted an exorcism that wasn't going well and issued an edict of this sort: "I command in the name of Jesus that the demon of [demon's name] be confined in a prison and be subject to Christ's judgment until such time as we shall call the spirit forth."

Specific angels may be summoned to deal with certain kinds of spirits. You may ask an angel of truth to torment a lying demon. Be as specific as necessary, but always understand that such a petition is subject to God's will. The Lord is Commander-in-Chief of heaven's armies, and it is His right to commission angels for earthly assistance. Don't depend upon angels instead of the Lord. Our primary dependence is upon the Lord Jesus, the use of prayer, the presence of the Holy Spirit, and the Word of God.

4. Call Forth Undesignated Demons

Most exorcists encounter times when we aren't sure what to do next. For instance, our knowledge of the demonic network may be limited in the early stages when there is uncertainty about the ranking of the demons. What demons should be commanded to manifest under these circumstances?

The Holy Spirit has taught me a tactic that has been successful in breaking through this barrier. I sometimes employ this trick of the trade to initiate an exorcism if I have no idea what demons are present. I say, "I command to come forth whatever spirit the Lord Jesus has identified to face divine judgment for violating this soul."

After speaking those words, a demon almost always manifests. Then I check to see whether or not this is an interfering spirit. I say, "Are you the demon that *Jesus Christ* has specifically called forth for judgment?"

If the demon acknowledges he isn't the right spirit, command him to be punished for interfering, and then tell him to recede and make way for the correct demon. Do this several times until the specific demon, the one God wants dealt with, comes forward.

Deeper into the exorcism the log can be consulted to decide which demon is next in the succession to be cast out. Even with a detailed log I sometimes ask for the one God wants dealt with, because I sense some spirit needs to be confronted that may not have been previously identified. By summoning the one whom God has appointed to judgment, I am always certain that the time to confront each demon is accurate.

5. Find the Function of the Demon

Knowing the demon's function may be the most important information to understanding how a particular evil spirit should be handled. This puts the exorcist in sync with the parameters for handling each spirit. If the demon is a mind-control spirit, then the exorcist will know to be aware of mind games and intellectual trickery. If the spirit has a name indicating more visceral responses (murder or violence, for instance), the exorcist will be on guard against physical retaliation and also the possibility that the person or his ancestors have committed some violent act.

Knowing the function of the spirit will help the exorcist discover the demon's legal grounds. An example would be a demon of incest. If the victim has said nothing about such a moral dilemma, the chances are the incest demon is exploiting an event that the victim may have denied or suppressed.

It is sometimes advisable to cut the demon off from his function. For example, a demon of false wisdom could be a powerful spirit whose intellectual acumen is crucial to the demonic system. In that case, I would pray, "I take the sword of the Spirit and cut off False Wisdom from his function. I separate the demon from his ability to think and act wisely in the interests of Satan. Having removed the demon from his wisdom, I command that this spirit become foolish and unlearned, and exhibit traits contrary to his function."

Be aware that the function of the demon may not be designated by the demon's actual name. Sometimes the function is hidden because the demon knows that this information will point toward the legal ground by which he remains. A case in point would be a demon of murder. The exorcist might think such a demon's function would be to kill someone. However, murder might also be defined as destroying the emotional capacities of the person, "murdering" their soulish sensitivities. A demon of self-hate might function in several different ways. This kind of spirit could cause masochistic mutilation or influence homosexual behavior. In the first instance the mutilation would be a physical means of demonstrating self-hate. In the second instance the homosexual behavior would be a way of rejecting one's true sexual identity as a means of self-loathing.

6. Employ the Assistance of the Victim

I have written this book from the perspective of the exorcist. The dialogue of each narrative has been shortened to provide the essence of the battles between myself and Satan's demons. I have not included my often lengthy conversations with the victims. In fact, a great portion of the time spent in many exorcisms is more devoted to talking with and ministering to the one under attack than confronting and rebuking the demons.

Victims are as much a part of the exorcism and a co-combattant as I am. Their assertions of moral and spiritual authority are crucial to their freedom. It is futile to tell a demon what to do, unless the command is backed up by the victim's agreement and aggressive resistance to Satan. The exorcism will be unsuccessful without these elements of cooperation.

At times when I have been stymied and uncertain of what to do next, God has often led the victim to suggest a course of action that proved to be the key to lasting victory. I always carefully listen to what the victim has said, because the person is often used by God as much as I am to confront the indwelling demons. Sometimes a victim has said, "This may sound crazy, but . . ." and has hesitated to continue. I encouraged the person to speak whatever is on his or her mind and to let me, with the help of the Holy Spirit, sort out what to do.

An exorcism is an exercise in encouragement, as much as it is an attempt at expulsion. It's a critical opportunity to teach victims about their redeemed authority in Christ and their scriptural position as believers. I often pause during deliverance and give a brief Bible study to build up the victim's faith and understanding. I encourage questions so that they may settle any issues about who they are in Christ.

Demons may battle for control of the person's mind and fog his or her thinking so he or she cannot resist. "Focus your thoughts on Christ. Concentrate on the Resurrection. Quote from memory any Bible verses you know," I say to inspire the victim.

If the one receiving deliverance asked for a time of rest, I have tried to determine whether the person was wavering in his or her resolve or was genuinely in need of relief from the conflict. A victim's physical and spiritual vitality is necessary, and I am sensitive to the person's condition.

I often meet the victim for the first time prior to the exorcism. My travel schedule does not generally permit me to have a face-to-face follow-up relationship. Furthermore, I am not an academically trained counselor, and make no such claims of clinical expertise. My role is that of a spiritual warrior who skirmishes with Satan when he crosses my path, and the Lord leads me to minister to one who is demonized. I do, however, recognize the critical importance of ongoing professional assistance for those victims who have been freed.

Once a person has been delivered from demons, there are spiritual issues that will take time to resolve. An exorcism "specialist" such as myself may not be the best person to bond with the victim for future rehabilitation. Trained ministers and Christian psychologists who specialize in spiritual warfare need to take over and further assist in restoring mental and emotional health—a task that can take months or years.

Just as the cooperation of the victim was vital during an exorcism, the person's collaboration is important after the last demon is gone. The struggle to achieve freedom, as well as to maintain it, is a battle for the assertion of the victim's will. This goal will be reached by helping the person recognize that his or her spiritual self-esteem is grounded in Christ.

The victim's whole heart must be turned toward God, and the exorcist must carefully monitor every reaction and answer every concern. The one demonized is in the middle of the fight and can best see how Satan's punches are being thrown. He or she isn't like an anesthetized hospital patient, where the suffering one's thoughts and wishes are inconsequential to the success of the surgery. A deliverance isn't a one-man or one-woman operation. It's a team effort that requires a shoulder-to-shoulder solidarity that unites the exorcist and the victim in their common war against Satan.

7. Break All Curses

This topic has already been dealt with in regard to ancestral and generational curses, but I want to emphasize the importance of this rule as an integral part of dealing with relational curses. This form of spiritual bondage affects someone as the result of a marital, sexual, or soul-bonding relationship.

While ancestral and generational curses are implemented by blood relatives, spousal curses are also dangerous. Because the husband is head of the wife, his involvement in the occult could affect his marriage partner. A Christian woman married to an unbelieving man who dabbles in the occult should pray, "I submit to my husband according to the Scriptures, except in those cases where he claims a spiritually unlawful right. I break that occult bondage in the name of Jesus and refuse to submit to any forces of evil that would endanger my soul."

Couples involved in a sexual relationship outside of marriage have become one flesh and thus forge a union that can result in demonic subjection. For example, a man sexually cohabiting with a woman who is a witch could fall prey to the demons affecting her. If he comes to Christ, the sexual relationship must be ended and all soul-bonds (which are control mechanisms) broken through prayer. On a lesser level, strong friendships or social and business allegiances with someone involved in the occult could also affect an individual unaware.

Even though the exorcist might not suspect the victim has any ancestral, generational, or relational curses that need to be broken, there is no harm in addressing these issues as a matter of caution.

8. Force the Demon to Tell the Truth or Face Judgment

Scripture clearly indicates that Satan is a liar who cannot hold to the truth (John 8:44; Rev. 21:8). Can the exorcist, then, ever trust what a demon says? We must use spiritual discernment to determine the accuracy of any information provided by a demon. And we should never become involved in any irrelevant conversation. Demons will try to engage the exorcist in all kinds of dialogue as a delaying tactic.

I often say to demons, "I command that you only speak what God allows you to say, no more and no less. I command that you say nothing more than that which is permitted by God to facilitate your expulsion."

Having taken that precaution, how much do I believe of what a demon discloses? I weigh each statement carefully and test it against the Scriptures (1 John 4:1). I also verify the information by comparing it to the demon's other comments to see if it is consistent. I've discovered an additional procedure that has proven valuable. Instruct the demon this way: "I command that the answer you give be held accountable before almighty God and that you be judged if you lie to the Holy Spirit."

Most unclean spirits will be obedient to the truth after they hear this. However, I sometimes have to repeat this command several times. Some demons have such an acute propensity for prevarication that I have to parenthetically command them not to lie before every question and after every answer.

If I suspect a demon has lied to me, I respond, "I hold your answer up before God to be judged by His truth. If you have lied to the Holy Spirit, and if you have misled the servant of God, I ask God to smite you."

Words can't describe the terror I've seen on the faces of demons as God strikes them for their disobedience. They grimace, scream, cry out for mercy, and beg to be relieved from God's torment. Then I might say, "I ask God to stand back and give you another opportunity to speak the truth. If you do not, God will smite you again seven times greater."

Meticulously applying this tactic, often to the point of repetitious boredom, I force demons to abide in some measure of truth. I use the threat of God's judgment as often as necessary to make certain I'm not being misled.

9. Have the Victim Confess the Sin of Demonic Entry

We must keep in mind that God is dealing with the victim to grant freedom and growth. So we, also, must face the victim with personal responsibility to deal with issues in his or her own life. The victim must apply the truth of God's Word to obtain freedom from the bondage of Satan's lies.

Once a demon's presence, name, and function have been identified, the next step is to remove his right to remain. This is usually grounded in a conscious, willful sin. Have the victim renounce this sin and seek forgiveness through the blood of Christ by a spoken prayer. Demonic resistance is common, and I often have the victim say one word at a time. Just a few sentences of confession may take minutes, even hours. With others, it may come quite freely. This is the demon's stronghold, and he fights tenaciously to stop the prayer. In drastic situations I may halt the prayer to encourage the victim with Scriptures about forgiveness and God's grace.

At this point, distracting demons often interfere. Victims may become nauseous or experience shooting pains. Their minds may be so clouded, they barely know what is happening. I've had victims say things backward or convolute the wording of the prayer.

One woman who had been a high priestess in a mystery cult actually said words of praise to Satan, even though her lips were trying to form a prayer to God. The demonic stratagem was so effective, her ears heard godly words though she was speaking curses. I had to stop exorcising the demon and call forth the mental demon who was twisting her words; then I got rid of him so the prayer could proceed properly.

Sins of demonic entry aren't always acts of a specific place and time. There may be emotional harbors of evil, such as bitterness, jealousy, lust, or covetousness. You may not know the exact time the demon sufficiently exploited this area of life. No matter. Have the victim set the situation right with God. If the demon was misleading, it will soon become apparent. If the confession removes the right of entry, the demon's reaction will readily prove it. He will switch tactics; instead of claiming a legal right, he may start saying he won't leave regardless of what the exorcist does.

10. Make the Demon Pronounce His Own Doom

The exorcist may choose to speak the words of final expulsion, but the Holy Spirit has shown me a more effective way to weaken the demon's final attempt to stay. Have the demon pronounce his own doom. Recite the words and make the demon repeat them. This is the declaration of surrender I use: "I, [demon speaks his own name], acknowledge that Christ is Lord and has risen from the dead to defeat my master, the devil. I renounce all past, present, and future claims to [demon speaks name of his victim] and acknowledge that the one I possess has victory over me in the name of Jesus Christ. I bind to me all parts and portions of myself, and I attach to me any demons under my control. Having no further legal right to stay in this child of God, I lie not to the Holy Spirit, and I go now to the pit!"

Those few words may take many minutes. The demon may repeat phrases at first, but the last six words have to be spoken separately. I've spent an hour getting a demon to say the final word—*pit*.

However long it takes to enforce the capitulation, every moment is to be savored. The long struggle is over, the demon has been defeated, and Christ's promises have prevailed. Now memories of the long struggle fade away. The presence of God's Spirit is overwhelming. My eyes often fill with tears.

It's clear that Satan truly is "like a corpse trodden underfoot" (Isa. 14:19). Jesus has the keys to hell and death (Rev. 1:18) and no weapon formed against the child of God shall prosper (Isa. 54:17). Jesus has crushed Satan under the feet of those who bring the good news!

At the end of each successful exorcism, I am always deeply moved to witness Christ's finished work at the Cross. The mystery of the ages, that God loved fallen man so much He sent His Son "while we were still sinners" (Rom. 5:8), seems even more priceless. In the natural realm, angels (faithful and unfaithful) are more powerful and more intelligent than human beings. Yet God has mercifully chosen man, not angels, to be the objects of His grace.

It is Christians who are made "alive together with Christ" (Eph. 2:5) and allowed to "sit together in the heavenly places in Christ Jesus" (Eph. 2:6). While conditionally we do not always deserve such a lofty status, by positional right we are granted what mere human worthiness could never merit.

I once declared to a demon who threatened and taunted me, "In the name of Jesus, I command that you look at me. Gaze into my eyes and see into my soul. What do you see?"

"The righteousness of Jesus!" the evil spirit screamed in dismay. In the realm of spiritual warfare, the truth shines forth.

Christians often give lip service to the words of 1 John 4:4: "He who is in you is greater than he who is in the world." Experiencing an exorcism amplifies this truth. Casting out a demon is only possible because of the Resurrection. It is the empty tomb that allows us to face incomprehensible evil with certainty of victory and the authority of Christ in us, the "hope of glory" (Col. 1:27).

The exorcist, and the one to whom he ministers, are a team, united with Christ by the sacrifice of His blood. This union with the Savior forms a heavenly combination that no evil spirit can forever withstand. Demons try to run Christians off by reminding them of their fallen nature; but it is the new life in Jesus by which we have been "raised with Christ" (Col. 3:1) that causes evil spirits to flee.

Every believer who has been victimized by the devil needs to acknowledge that no matter what failures beset a believer, the born-again Christian is seated at God's right hand. Knowing who you are in Christ and where you are positioned in His kingdom is a spiritual reality that is sure to doom every demon to defeat.

CHAPTER 14

† *Restoration in the Name of Jesus*

I had been doing exorcisms for only a few years when I met fourteen-year-old Brenda. She spoke to me in the hallway of a Baptist church where I had just concluded a four-day series of lectures. At that time this church was one of the largest in America, and their invitation to speak was an opportunity to expand my ministry. If I received a good word of recommendation from the pastor, I'd be inundated with invitations. I had packed the sanctuary for each day of the seminar. Spiritually, I was elated and awaiting the pastor's endorsement.

"Can I speak to you privately about something?" Brenda asked. "It will only take a moment."

Since this was my last night at the church, many people wanted to shake my hand and express appreciation for my messages. I suspected Brenda wanted to do the same, so I motioned her to the side of the corridor, away from the flow of people.

"What's on your mind?" I asked.

Brenda dropped her eyes and stared at the floor. "It's hard for me to explain. It's embarrassing."

She was short, so I knelt and looked up into her face. Tears streamed from her eyes. "Take a deep breath and steady yourself," I suggested. "Go on when you feel comfortable."

Brenda sniffled and regained her composure. "I read pornography. I'm ashamed afterward, but I can't help myself. Sometimes when I read dirty magazines, I do things to myself I shouldn't. You know what I mean, don't you?"

Brenda's question was direct, but she averted her eyes. My heart was touched by her sincerity. *I'll pray with her and turn her over to the youth pastor to follow up,* I thought. *She was courageous to approach me all alone and talk about something so personal.*

"Brenda, I'd like to say a prayer for you and ask someone to talk with you further. Would that be okay?"

Brenda nodded. "You can tell them about the pornography, but please don't tell them about . . ."

"About what?" I asked.

Brenda closed her eyes and waved her hand across her face with a "never mind" gesture.

"Don't worry," I assured her. "I won't say anything more than you want me to. Take my hand while I pray."

Still kneeling, I reached up and clasped her right hand in mine. "Dear Lord Jesus," I prayed, "thank You for Brenda's honesty, and her desire to deal with this problem. I ask You to cover her in Your blood and—"

"No-o-o-o-o!" The word interrupted my prayer.

I wasn't sure I heard correctly. The "no" sounded like a groan from inside Brenda's body. I opened my eyes and continued. "Lord, I know You love Brenda and will help her overcome this sin, because You are the Son of God and rose victoriously from the dead—"

"No He didn't!" Another interruption, and this time a scowl appeared on Brenda's face. The words were drawn out in a growl. Her bowed head tilted up, and that look filled her eyes.

I glanced around and saw people were milling about the hallway, exchanging greetings. I didn't want to cause any commotion that would embarrass Brenda, so I took control over the demon. "Whoever you are, I bind you in the name of Jesus. Go down now, until such time as I call you forth again."

The voice said nothing, but the glare from Brenda's eyes spoke volumes. The demon blinked a couple of times, and then Brenda returned.

I stood from my kneeling position and motioned for her to follow me. "I think we need to talk a little more," I explained. "There's an empty room around the corner. Wait there, and I'll be back in a few minutes."

The pastor's office was at the other end of the hallway, so I could keep an eye on the door to Brenda's room. When I arrived at the pastor's office, he was talking to the youth pastor.

"Bob, great message tonight," the pastor said and patted me on the shoulder. "We were just discussing how much we'd like to have you back. That crowd tonight was one of the biggest we've ever had; I think you'll be very pleased at the love offering for your ministry."

"Thank you, that's very kind." I paused, unsure of how to express what I had to say. "I've encountered a situation that I think you'll be interested in," I said, and turned toward the youth pastor. "Do you know a teenager in your church named Brenda?"

"Sure, if it's the same Brenda I'm thinking of. She's short with auburn hair and blue eyes." He looked at the pastor. "Joe's daughter."

"Oh, yes," the pastor acknowledged. "Her dad is one of our deacons. Why do you ask? She's one of my best soul-winners."

This won't go over well, I thought. "Pastor, do you mind if I bring her to your office for a few minutes? This is a difficult situation."

He shrugged his shoulders.

"I'll be right back," I said as I walked away.

I returned to the room where Brenda was waiting and asked her to follow me. I would have summoned her father, but this exorcism occurred before I learned how important it is for parents to be present during a child's exorcism. When we reached the pastor's office, Brenda stopped. "I can't go in there and tell him what I've told you. My dad is a . . ."

"A deacon. Don't worry. I already know. I don't want to embarrass you, but you have some very serious spiritual problems, and I feel your pastor and youth pastor need to be present for our discussion. I trust these brothers in Christ."

Brenda's face was flushed and I could tell she wanted to walk away, but she drew in a breath and nodded her head. We knocked on the door, and the pastor opened it. He gave Brenda a shoulder hug and invited us inside. I sat next to Brenda on the couch while the pastor and youth pastor sat opposite us. "Brenda has confided a problem to me, and I'd like the four of us to pray together so she'll have spiritual victory. She may not want to discuss what bothers her right now, but the Lord knows and He'll hear our prayer."

The pastor smiled. "Absolutely. Lead us in prayer," he suggested, motioning toward me.

I nodded and they bowed their heads. I hadn't told Brenda that she had a demon, so she wasn't apprehensive about doing as I asked. I looked at her and began praying. "Our Father in heaven, we come in the authority of Jesus, the name above every name. Thank You that by the power of Your Son's blood we can overcome any sin."

I paused. Nothing happened. Where was the demon who confronted me moments ago, when I had mentioned the blood of Christ?

"Jesus, thank You for defeating the devil at the Cross."

Still nothing. *I'm glad I didn't tell them she had a demon,* I thought. *Maybe Brenda was up to some trick and fooled me.*

I continued my prayer. "Brenda needs to defeat this sin in her life, and I ask You to give her a new filling of your Holy Spirit and—"

All at once the voice broke in. "There is no Holy Spirit!"

The snarl was clearly from another entity. The eyes of the pastor and youth pastor widened, and they both straightened in their chairs. The youth pastor leaned toward Brenda.

Now the truth is going to be known, I thought. "Who said there is no Holy Spirit? I command, in the name of Jesus, that you tell me who you are!"

Brenda's head tilted up and the demon fully manifested. "I did."

"What's your name?"

"Lust. You can't make me leave. I have a legal right to this body!"

Brenda's mannerisms were gone, and a male personality

came over her. Her eyes changed and so did her gestures and expressions.

The pastors watched intently, but said nothing. I felt the presence of God leading me, and went forward in faith. I proceeded to bind Lust and call forth Brenda. Carefully, I explained to her that she had a demon, and that I needed her cooperation. She said she wanted to be free more than anything, so I continued the exorcism. For nearly an hour I battled the demon of lust, who said he had entered through Brenda's reading of pornography. Methodically, I led her in a prayer of confession regarding her sin; I was sure this would close the door on the demon's right to her.

During the hour I paused several times to ask the pastor if he had any questions or wanted to help in any way. Each time he shook his head and politely told me to continue doing whatever I felt I needed to do.

I longed for prayer support from either of the two men. But despite their lack of involvement, the deliverance went well. Lust put up a fight, but it was mostly intellectual and not physical. The exorcism was done with surprising calm and orderliness. I felt grateful that I didn't have to do something unorthodox that might have raised theological questions. Still, I was getting more uncomfortable by the minute.

"I, Lust, renounce my claim to Brenda, and leave now and go to the pit," I instructed the demon to say.

Lust resisted angrily. Brenda was thrown back and forth on the couch. I did my best to hold her arms firmly. Her legs kicked and her head shook furiously, but the pastors did not intervene. I kept her from harming herself or me, but the pastors continued to shrink from the conflict.

"Leave now and go to the pit!" I insisted over and over.

At last, Lust groaned, sighed, and Brenda's body went limp. I propped her against a couple of pillows and waited for her to come around. I looked at the pastor and then at the youth pastor. They did not move toward Brenda to comfort her, nor did they smile with relief at Christ's victory. They sat silently, observing.

This isn't the way most exorcisms end. Usually, the room is filled with exhausted elation. Those involved in the deliverance hug each other or cry. The tension fades as everyone looks at one another like human beings again. The long hours of hearing God's name constantly cursed have thankfully ended.

Brenda regained her composure, and her face was radiant. "Is it over?" she asked.

"I think so. It certainly seems that way, but just to be sure I always—"

"Brenda," the pastor interjected as he stood, "I know your parents must be very worried about you." He reached out for her hand to help her from the couch. "Come with me. We'll call and tell them you were talking with some young people and forgot about the time. I'll drive you home."

"Pastor," I said, "I think we should take a few minutes to see if everything is all right before Brenda leaves. Besides, there are some important instructions I have for her. If you don't mind I'd like to—"

"I do mind," he said firmly with an unsmiling expression. "It's late, and Brenda needs to go home now."

"May I talk with her parents when you call?" I asked.

"No, it's best that I speak with them, as their pastor."

"But I need to explain a little about what happened tonight so they'll know how to help Brenda."

The pastor's face turned stern. "There's no need to tell them anything that went on. What happened in my office doesn't leave this office. Do you understand?" He grabbed Brenda's hand. He looked at me and then at the youth pastor.

The young minister nodded his head in obedience. The pastor was twenty years my senior and one of the most respected church-builders in America, but I stood my ground. If he was advocating some kind of denial, I wasn't going along with it.

"The demon of lust might not be gone," I said. "If he isn't, her problems will be a lot worse since he has been antagonized and threatened. It will only take a few minutes to check for sure. I'm very concerned about her."

Brenda pulled her hand away from her pastor and looked at him, then at me. "If you think it will make a difference, I'll stay. I don't want that evil thing around." She walked back to the couch and sat down. "What do you want me to do?"

"The same thing you've been doing all evening. Listen carefully to what I say, cooperate with all your heart, and pray that Jesus will set you free."

The pastor stood motionless.

Brenda took a deep breath and closed her eyes. "I'm ready. Go ahead."

Why was I so insistent on not letting Brenda leave without further spiritual investigation?

WHAT TO DO WHEN AN EXORCISM HAS ENDED

In a significant number of exorcisms I've conducted, demons went through all the actions of being cast out, but they didn't go. Consequently, I've learned that when an exorcism seems to be over, it's still wise to check, recheck, and then check again to be sure the demon is truly gone. This is not a time for wishful thinking, hoping that everything is okay.

You should ask the victim how he or she feels. This person knows what it is like to have that demon around, and he or she is the best one to evaluate whether the spirit is gone. Ask the victim repeatedly if he or she senses any presence of the demon. The victim may feel hollow inside, because evil once filled spaces now empty in his or her soul. If the victim has any misgivings about freedom, it's better to err on the side of caution.

One way to find out if the demon is still present is to pray for the victim's complete filling of the Holy Spirit. Treat the body as the temple of the Holy Spirit. Dedicate each section of the body to Christ (Rom. 6:12–13). Ask the Lord to force into the open any evil part left behind and to indicate what area of the mind or body the demons might yet try to control. Be thorough. Take time to complete a spiritual diagnostic follow-up before the fruits of victory are fully savored.

Brenda's Demon Returns

During the follow-up procedure I knelt before Brenda and addressed the demon again. "Lust, I commanded you to leave in the name of Jesus. If you have disobeyed, I demand that you come to attention."

Nothing happened. The pastors stood by the door looking exasperated, and it appeared that my extra effort was foolish. It was obvious they weren't in agreement, so I tossed theological caution aside.

"Lord, I ask You to send strong angels. If Lust hasn't left, may Your angels torment him until he obeys."

Brenda's body jerked, and Lust groaned. He manifested with fury in his eyes.

"Leave me alone! I don't have to go."

"Yes, you do. I commanded you to leave."

"I don't have to leave if I have a right to stay."

"But Brenda confessed her sin of reading pornography. That's how you said you possessed her."

"True."

"Then, in Jesus' name I command that you tell me what else we need to know to set her free. May the angels of God torment you more until you quit misleading us."

Lust squirmed in agony. "Okay, okay. Call them off. I'll tell you."

"What's the legal right allowing you to stay?"

"Her father. He's the one."

"The one what?"

"The one who gave her the pornography. He left it lying around the house when she was a little girl. She tried to imitate what she saw in those pictures." The demon looked up at the pastor. "And he's your deacon," the spirit taunted.

That night was one of the most unpleasant I've ever spent. In spite of his reluctance, the angry pastor had no choice but to call the deacon to his office and confront him about the spirit's claims. The proof of what the demon said was the father's contrite admission that he harbored a craving for pornography. I ministered to the father who wept bitterly over his sin. Complete victory came when I led the father in a prayer to cast the demon out of his daughter.

When the exorcism was over, the pastor wouldn't look at me, but he allowed me to spend valuable time cautioning Brenda's father about how to help her heal effectively. Her father thanked me wholeheartedly for the deliverance. He seemed embarrassed in front of the pastor, and the two avoided each other.

The Aftermath of an Exorcism

I explained to Brenda's father that after an exorcism the victim needs special physical recuperation. He or she may sleep for twelve hours or more. The person may awaken the next day with external bruises and internal pain from the actions of the demon who has torn him or her inside (Mark 9:26). The victim is often dehydrated and hungry and will need extra liquids and food.

Emotional rehabilitation is also crucial. A mature counselor should monitor the victim's mental health to address every area of spiritual vulnerability. Some victims will be left with an emotional maturity that is many years younger than their age because they have been spiritually stunted. Those around them need to be supportive and understanding.

Demons of lust, perversion, addiction, and other forms of carnality leave their victims susceptible to the frailties that were points of demonic entry. These areas need to addressed with a Scripture memory program and serious Bible study. The demon may have been cast out, but the flesh still needs to be overcome daily through trust in God's Word.

If there were demons of rebellion, witchcraft, heresy, or false religions, a dose of strong orthodox Bible doctrine is necessary. The victim must quickly become immersed in teaching that confronts these "doctrines of demons" (1 Tim. 4:1). Banishing error isn't enough. The absorption of truth is crucial to the victim's recovery from the lies he or she once believed.

Those involved in the exorcism face unique challenges following a deliverance. After an initial sharing of the more dramatic aspects of what happened, the discussion should center on positive deliberations about God and His attributes. The spectacular feats of the enemy should not be the focus of the discussions. This tendency is hard to overcome, since some involved in the exorcism may have witnessed this demonic world for the first time. Let them briefly express their amazement, and then turn the emphasis toward what Christ has done. Before the group dismisses, a time of praise and thanksgiving to God is important. The next few days should be spent, as much as possible, in Scripture reading and quiet contemplation upon the Lord.

The most serious warning to those involved in an exorcism is to be wary of temptations and discouragement. One might think that after such a supernatural experience, they would be on a spiritual high. That exhilaration is short-lived. Satan strikes in such circumstances because he is unexpected. It was shortly after Elijah's great victory over the prophets of Baal on Mount Carmel (1 Kings 18:38–40) that he languished in dejection and asked God to take his life (1 Kings 19:4). I can testify that some of my most difficult struggles occurred after a triumphant exorcism. My emotional and physical exhaustion played into the devil's hands. I have since learned the importance of spiritual vigilance at such times.

The Illusion of Continued Possession

Can demons return once they are cast out? Those Christ sends to the pit are unable to escape to return. If not cast into the pit, they may reenter under any of three conditions: (1) there was some legal right left (as in Brenda's case), (2) the victim failed to fill his life with God's Spirit and truth, or (3) the victim returned to the same sin that permitted the original possession. Of course, different spirits, other than those cast out, may seek entrance.

I have also encountered another phenomenon that is a copycat of possession, which I call "demonic psychological imprinting." While the demon was internalized, he learned the mental processes of the victim's mind, in the same way a student of neurolinguistics programming masters the detection of physical and emotional patterns. In certain cases after deliverance, the demon can trigger psycho physiological responses that mimic possession. The demon, though outside, can affect the mind to such an extent that he appears to speak through the vocal cords. The evil spirit uses demonic oppression to trigger past mental patterns to which the victim is still susceptible. The victim may even feel repossessed, but it is an illusion that must be overcome by trust in God's power to keep those who abide in Him free.

The Patient Progress of Healing

Almost invariably, past victims become discouraged by how long spiritual reconstruction takes. Although they are exhilarated by the feeling of being freed, they become disheartened when their progress toward spiritual well-being isn't rapid. They must understand that Satan spent months, even years, dismantling the person God meant them to be. In place of their divinely given identity, the devil erected a complex caricature based on carnal impulses and selfish motivation. These negative patterns of behavior have to be reversed through spiritual reconditioning.

Imagine you were told to dismantle the General Motors

Corporation. Do you think that by walking into the offices of GM's executives and firing them, you could disassemble a multibillion-dollar organization immediately? Of course not. It would take time to close all the departments, manufacturing plants, and branch offices. Tearing down the infrastructure of evil in the victim's soul and body can be an equally arduous task, except in rare occasions.

One time as I counseled a victim of possession in the aftermath of her deliverance, the Lord brought to my mind Deuteronomy 7:22: "And the LORD your God will drive out those nations before you little by little; you will be unable to destroy them at once, lest the beasts of the field become too numerous for you." The children of Israel didn't defeat all the enemy at once. As they conquered each city, they settled the land and domesticated their surroundings. Once their holdings were consolidated, they moved on to another enemy and followed the same pattern.

This describes the process of deliverance as well as the pace of spiritual reconstruction after an exorcism. Instead of defeating every demon instantly, deliverance comes "little by little." Healing from all that the devil has done must come in God's timing and His way if spiritual rehabilitation is to be complete. In many instances, the assistance of Christian mental health professionals should be sought to further enhance the victim's psychological welfare.

Deliverance Isn't a Deed

Deliverance isn't a deed; it's a necessary step in total recuperation. Acts 10:38 says that Jesus "went about doing good and *healing* all who were oppressed by the devil" (emphasis added). The goal of an exorcism is not demonic eviction alone. It is also restoration of the victim's soul and body to spiritual wholeness so that they may once again be the person God meant them to be. Ministering healing is as important as bringing emancipation from the forces of darkness.

The entire body of Christ needs to be sensitive to this truth. Often, those delivered from demons find they are ostracized as spiritual lepers. Some Christians cruelly say that the victim was at fault for what happened (which isn't always the case), and therefore must have some inherent weakness that could rub off by association. Others argue mistakenly that the victim might still have demons around that could affect anyone who befriends that person.

But restoring the victim of possession to spiritual wholeness is the responsibility of the church, both local and universal. Real emotional and spiritual healing come when we in the body of Christ humble ourselves, confess our faults to one another (James 5:16), and realize we are all sinners saved by grace. By reaching out to those who have been ravaged by Satan's legions, Christians can serve Christ by extending His compassion "to the least of these," the most hurting among us (Matt. 25:40).

Brenda's Epilogue

When I said farewell to Brenda and her father, I was deeply troubled in my spirit. The pastor seemed outright antagonistic. I suspected he was theologically disturbed by the exorcism and professionally embarrassed by having to deal with the moral failures of a trusted deacon. In my mind's eye I can still see him standing in the doorway as we left, saying to everyone, "Remember, not a word of what's happened leaves this room. We must not say anything to anyone!"

But what happened did leak out. Perhaps someone overheard the demon's groans in the hallway or someone eavesdropped on the exorcism. The controversy that erupted in the days following besieged the pastor. Finally, he publicly addressed the issue from the pulpit the next Sunday morning.

I wasn't there, but a parishioner sent me a cassette tape of that sermon. When it arrived at my Denver headquarters a few days later, I put the cassette in a tape deck.

"Some of you have heard about an alleged exorcism that occurred at the church last week," the pastor said. "Yes, some very strange things happened, but let me assure you that the theological position of this church hasn't changed. Jesus cast out demons to prove He was the Son of God, and that sort of thing ended with the apostolic age. We don't deal with demons here, and we don't want people around who do. If you think you have a demon, go somewhere else. Our job is to win souls to Christ, not perform exorcisms!"

I hit the off button on the recorder and slammed my fist on the desk. "God, how could You let this happen?" I cried out. "Is this the thanks I get for helping Brenda? Now I'll never speak in a large church like that one again."

I paced the floor in frustration. *What about Brenda?* I thought. *I wonder how she felt after that sermon? She and her father must be horrified. Maybe they doubt what happened. If they do, will the demons exploit their unbelief and find a way to come back?*

My feelings were a mixture of sincere concern for Brenda's spiritual welfare and a selfish reaction to my ego having been bruised.

For the next week I never picked up my Bible. I didn't pray. I was angry with God and my fellowship with Him suffered. I may have defeated the demon in Brenda, but I couldn't conquer my own spirit. I was drifting farther and farther away from the Lord, so far that I considered quitting Christian service. Unlike Elijah, I didn't want to die. I didn't have to. I already felt dead spiritually.

Ten days after Brenda's exorcism, a letter from her arrived in the mail.

Dear Mr. Larson,

There are no words to describe how grateful I am for all that you did for me. Slowly, I've been remembering what I went through that night in my pastor's office. I still don't understand all that happened, but I know how I felt when it was over. I still feel the same. . . .

I haven't touched a single dirty magazine since that night, and I haven't done that bad thing again. My dad and I have become best friends. We pray and read the Bible together every day. He has changed so much. Mom and he are more in love than ever. She has forgiven him. . . .

Tears were streaming down my cheeks. I felt humbled and ashamed.

A lot of people have questions about that night. I just tell them that Bob Larson is the most special person in the world, and that God used you to do some really neat things for me. Thank you for letting God use you. I'll always love Jesus because you cared enough to help me.

Brenda

Brenda had done as much to minister to me as I had done to minister to her and her dad. I put the letter aside and buried my face in my hands. I asked God's forgiveness for my sins of arrogance and self-centeredness.

In the midst of my sorrow Galatians 1:10 came to mind: "If I still pleased men, I would not be a bondservant of Christ."

"Jesus," I cried out. "I'll never again turn my back on someone who is bound by Satan, if You tell me to help them."

What is the legacy of the day in Singapore when I faced my first demon, and that day I read Brenda's letter? I have kept my promise to minister deliverance to those hurting souls God sends to me. I've not been able to help everyone who has crossed my path, and I haven't always had the opportunity to help everyone as much as I wanted. But when God has clearly spoken to my heart to deal with a demon, I've never backed down.

Satan has waged a ferocious counterattack. I have been publicly humiliated by those who said they were doing God a service. I have felt the demons of hell surround me and move in for the kill. My heart has been immeasurably hurt and my spirit has been nearly broken by the lies and deceit of the enemy. And like every Christian, I've failed God more times than I want to admit.

In retaliation for what I've done to the devil, he has struck back to take from me some things I cherished. But the Lord has never allowed Satan to rob me of the things that mattered most: the fellowship of true friends, the love of family, and the grace of God that has kept me in His hands.

I've been blessed! With great suffering has come even greater spiritual bounty. Yes, I have been battered, but I'm still standing, still serving, and still casting out demons *in the name of Jesus.*

ABOUT THE AUTHOR

Bob Larson is the host of a daily one-hour show, Bob Larson Live, heard in approximately 150 cities in the United States and Canada. He has lectured in more than seventy countries and has appeared on such television shows as *The Oprah Winfrey Show*, *The Phil Donahue Show*, *Montel*, *Sally Jesse*, and *Larry King Live*.

Larson is the author of twenty-four books, including the novels *Dead Air*, *Abaddon*, and *The Senator's Agenda*, as well as *Satanism: The Seduction of America's Youth*, *Straight Answers on the New Age*, and *Larson's New Book of Cults*.

Other books
from Bob Larson

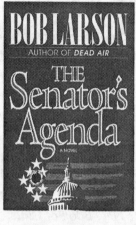

The Senator's Agenda
A Novel

Wes Bryant wages war with his conscience in a no-holds-barred battle to discover the truth about the Senator's agenda at all costs and against all odds.

0-7852-7879-6 • Hardcover • 288 pages

Dead Air
A Novel

A chilling bestselling novel of one man's struggle to overcome evil with good. Wes Bryant is a small town radio talk show host whose life is fairly quiet. But when a young child calls into the station, asking for help from the man who keeps tormenting her, Bryant's life is thrown into a tailspin of intrigue, horror, and life-threatening danger.

0-8407-7638-1 • Paperback • 352 pages

Straight Answers On the New Age

This comprehensive Christian appraisal of the New Age movement stands as the definitive reference work for clergy and laity who need to know the potential dangers of these radical beliefs. Answers to commonly asked questions follow each topical overview along with a mini-glossary of people, places and terms associated with the subject.

0-8407-3032-2 • Paperback • 288 pages